SUPERHEROES WEAR MOM JEANS

To Dru —
A Superhero!
— Susie

SUPERHEROES WEAR MOM JEANS

The Tangled Ball®
Guide to Anti-Bullying for
Parents of Young Children

Susan S. Raisch

Tangled Ball Books

*If the game of life is about
laughter and love...we won.*

For Ken

And for the four children
who became our Go-To Adults:
Alice-Kate, Peter, Molly, Jack

For their Go-To Adults: Brandy, Sarah, Tom

And for our future little leaders: Lucy and Felix

CONTENTS

What Is a Tangled Ball®?

Bullying is messy and complicated. In other words, it's a tangled ball of unpredictable behavior—perpetually challenging for children and parents alike. And although there's no "one size fits all" solution, no child who faces bullying should ever feel alone or diminished.

That means anti-bullying requires leadership, first on the part of a parent, and then, as children come of age, through their own strength and character.

Tangled Ball® is about untangling the multiple factors involved, one string at a time. Our mission is to help promote the best messages and the most effective tools to recognize it at its core and to deal with it effectively on every level, from the playground to our computers at home.

As we unravel the strings of this tangled ball, we discover the merits and never-ending value of self-awareness, empathy, empowerment, education, communication, parent involvement, school climate, and skill development.

The goal of Tangled Ball® is to help anyone who has a stake in the welfare of children to untangle the problems of bullying—one string at a time.

For more information, keep reading—and please visit www.tangledball.com.

Introduction

My son and I stared in horror at the television as events played out at Columbine High School in Colorado. It was April 1999, and as Peter and I watched a bloodied teenage boy dangling from a broken window, clinging to life, we had no idea that 12 of his peers and one teacher lay dead inside the building, while many others were already severely wounded and traumatized. All of them, and probably most of their small community, were changed for life as a result of that day.

As soon as we found out that the two students who were responsible for this unimaginable tragedy had taken their own lives, I could blurt out only a single word.

"Why?"

"They must have been bullied," Peter said, with no hesitation.

"How do you know?" I said.

"Mom, it happens all the time," he said.

"Is it really that bad?" I naively asked.

Peter nodded.

With the help of time, research, and several books, such as Dave Cullen's *Columbine* or Sue Klebold's *A Mother's Reckoning: Living in the Aftermath of Tragedy*, we now understand that mental illness was most likely a core reason for the violence that occurred at Columbine High School. To be clear, it would be unfair to continue the myth that this horrible act was a direct result of bullying. But the fact that most other teens I asked at the time *assumed* it was bullying became a big deal to me, and to other parents, as well.

Maybe you were a teen back then in 1999, and you have young children of your own now. You may have been watching and experiencing something similar to what Peter and I did. I don't know about you or your parents, but it was clear to me that as adults and parents we did not—and still don't—fully comprehend what happens in our children's world.

But when we listen to them, guide them, laugh and cry with them, we have a powerful and positive impact on two vital points: how they feel about themselves and how they treat others in their world.

As a parent, I wanted to know more about the issue of bullying. I also felt the need to explore possible solutions. But first, I had questions:

What is bullying, and how and when does it start?

Bullying can take many forms, from physical (hitting or kicking) to verbal ("You're ugly!") or exclusionary ("You can't sit here!"). It is repeated aggressive behavior meant to make another person feel bad.

It is creating and/or taking advantage of an imbalance of power, whether it is physically, intellectually, misusing information to make someone feel embarrassed, or spreading rumors. If the desire is there, there are endless ways to make others feel really terrible about themselves.

When kids flex their social muscles early on it may not be considered bullying, at least not yet. In other words, the little tikes aren't necessarily bullies, but they are starting to behave as if they may soon deserve the label.

What is normal, age-appropriate behavior that needs to be corrected and what should be considered bullying?

"Bullying among young children is not uncommon," Dr. Ronald G. Slaby and Dr. Kim Storey revealed in a 2008 curriculum introduction called *The Eyes on Bullying Program.* "When groups of young children, who often differ significantly in physical size, skill level, and family experience, get together regularly, patterns of hurtful behavior often emerge. Children make mean faces, say threatening things, grab objects, push others aside, falsely accuse, or refuse to play with others.

"These behaviors are precursors to verbal, physical, or indirect bullying—though they are not always recognized as such. Some young children are also capable of engaging in actual bullying behaviors by deliberately and repeatedly dominating a more vulnerable peer through name-calling, physical attacks, and social exclusion."[1]

We can safely assume that if this type of behavior goes unchecked, little kids testing the waters may turn into bigger kids who don't know how to act differently.

Dan Olweus, PhD, founder of the Olweus Bullying Prevention Program, says in *Bullying at School: What We Know and What We Can Do*, "The guiding rule of action should be to intervene too early rather than too late."

It's hard to argue with his assessment. In other words, as the Tangled Ball® philosophy describes, the strings of childhood get tangled early on and it behooves us adults to get in the mix *before* things get too tangled.

So if you are a parent, or perhaps a grandparent of young children, or maybe a teacher of kids by trade, I'd like to help. Over the past few years, I have been on a journey to learn as much as possible about specific things within a parent or adult's capability that can help children achieve a feeling of safety and wholeness.

Now I'd like to share what I have learned with you— the superhero—one of the most powerful people in your child's life. That's right. You *are* a superhero to your kids, at least in their early years of development. That's exactly when we need to begin paying attention to the risks inherent in childhood behavior. By first taking an active stance in recognizing bullying—cue the superhero—we increase our chances of figuring out appropriate and effective ways to combat it.

I wrote this book to remind parents of young children that although shielding children completely from mean behavior may not be possible, it is fully within our abilities to play the most important role as skilled and trusted adults.

As we all find out in due time, parenting is sloppy. If

---

[1] Slaby, R.G., Storey, K.S. (2008), *The Eyes on Bullying Program* (online).

we could order a crystal ball online that could tell us that they will survive and thrive in this imperfect world, the delivery trucks would be working overtime.

In other words, we hope every day that we're not messing them up. We can't hold ourselves to some perfect standard, but in hindsight there are some basics that can help keep the wheels securely on for the long haul. And we shouldn't overlook the fact that how we parent our own children directly affects how other children fare, as well.

While raising my own young children, I worked as a publicist in the television and publishing industries. The companies and projects I worked on ranged from MTV to Sesame Street to the History Channel (now referred to as HISTORY) and a lot in between.

See a pattern? I started out cool, became a mom of four kids, and eventually became uncool. (Just kidding. History is cool.)

At the time of the Columbine shootings, I was consulting at ABC News, and while the coverage of that story faded my interest did not. I've spent the past several years attending multiple conferences, reading countless books and talking to experts, including professionals in the fields of bullying prevention, leadership, psychology and early child development, as well as school counselors, principals, teachers, and parents. Most important, I've spent a significant amount of time trying to figure this out directly with kids.

Here's what I've I learned so far:

1. Bullying is complicated. It's a tangled ball. No two situations are the same and it's almost impossible to give "one size fits all" advice.
2. Although not all situations can be classified as "bullying," mean behavior starts young and can create a long tail of pain.
3. The role of the parent is critical. The "Go-To Trusted Adult" is the difference between mean behavior being a bump in the road or a child lugging around that long tail of pain.
4. It's not just about prevention; it's about being

proactive. It's about nurturing little leaders who can handle messy situations.

5. Parents don't need a degree in psychology or early childhood development to become a good Go-To Trusted Adult. All we need is to pay attention, suspend judgment, yield to empathy, and consult with experts when we're not sure if following our basic intuitions is the best option.

6. Parents can be superheroes—even in mom jeans and dad sneakers—but kids won't know it firsthand until they are superhero parents, too.

As Robert Fulgham said in his landmark book, *All I Really Need to Know I Learned in Kindergarten,* "You may never have proof of your importance but you are more important than you think. There are always those who couldn't do without you. The rub is that you don't always know who."

I'm here to tell you that it's your own kids.

As adults, we need to believe in and listen to our own instincts as well as discover and believe in the unique strengths of our children. Even geniuses need the advice of others to get the best results.

Rick Ackerly, educator, parent, grandparent, and author of *The Genius in Children: Encouraging Character, Curiosity and Creativity in Children,* whose work is based on the theory that all children have an internal compass that, when nurtured correctly, helps them find their authentic and best self, says that "Genius is the teacher within all of us. It is the *you* that is becoming. It is our inner author and our source of our authority in the world."

So while this process takes time, just like growing into parenting, learning how to interact successfully with others starts young, which is why this book was written for parents and teachers of pre-K through elementary school. Just like any long distance run, starting strong has a lot to do with a strong finish and it's important that you never underestimate your own power.

Being in charge of children isn't easy under the best of

circumstances. When they feel diminished, confused, angry, or alone and aren't performing to their potential, it can make our heads spin and our hearts ache. When you are facing a challenging situation with your child, it's vital to first preserve your own sanity. That way, you will be better equipped to untangle the problem—one string at a time—so that you can really help your child become his or her best.

If *you* don't, then who will?

Or, as the great Lily Tomlin once put it, "I always wondered why somebody doesn't do something about that. Then I realized I was somebody."

We're *all* that somebody.

By choosing to read this book, you're taking responsibility for another key aspect of your children's welfare. In this case, it's the prospect—or the existence—of bullying.

It took me at least ten years of thinking about this harsh problem before I finally decided to give up my career in publicity and spend most of my time on the issue of bullying prevention. As a result, I started Tangled Ball®, a consulting service aimed at promoting high-quality information to homes and schools, but it's the kids who teach us the most.

Of course with such access to good information, you would think that I would have instantly known how to respond when a fourth grader sat next to me during a school visit and poured his heart out.

Wrong.

Sam didn't know me at all but he had to tell someone how tortured he felt. Another boy in his class was making it his mission to put him down at every opportunity and was egging on others to do the same. The facts of Sam's story were undoubtedly not good, but listening to the tone of his voice and seeing his face as he spoke was breaking my heart and I was panicking inside. I didn't want to say the wrong thing. Of course, since I'm not a trained counselor, I asked him if he wanted to talk to someone like that.

For the moment, at least, he chose me. I'm not sure why, but maybe he just had a feeling that I was interested.

I tried to be totally present and to continue making eye contact so that he would feel as if he was my only focus and I wasn't going anywhere. Although talking wasn't as important as listening, I had to say something when he finished. The only thing I could come up with is what I think I would have wanted to hear if I were his age and struggling with a similar situation.

"That's terrible!" I said. "You don't deserve that."

I knew enough not to offer any quick solutions. He seemed to relax. We talked about how he could bring up the subject with his parents or one of his teachers or with the school counselor, but at that precise moment Sam simply needed to feel that someone was paying attention.

I thought of the words from my favorite award-winning children's book, *One*, by Kathryn Otoshi: "Sometimes It Just Takes One."

That's where you might come in.

The most common piece of advice that bullying prevention experts tell children is "Tell a trusted adult." Like all of us, kids need to feel validated and supported. But there is a hitch. Most of us are well meaning, but can we be trusted? Do we know how to react? Sometimes our instincts are to say and do things that make it difficult for children to be forthcoming about challenging situations they are experiencing.

The stories and resources in this book have been chosen to help parents and all "Go-To Adults" work on specific skills so that kids have access to real help and can develop their own leadership skills.

We can accomplish that by keeping our eye on that prize. That comes from creating a culture of trust, empathy, common sense, and good communication as we prepare our children to handle the bumps in the road with skill and confidence.

For both parents and children, life can become a rollercoaster with unexpected twists and turns along the way—some of them exhilarating while others can be quite disturbing. Thank you for coming along for the ride.

When it comes to bullying, no child should ever feel alone.

It is totally within our reach to make a child feel important, even if someone in his or her peer group—or a sibling or even an adult—gives a totally opposite message. (Sad to say, but it's not just kids who can be mean.)

There are many strings that make up the tangled ball of a child's existence and some of them can jeopardize an emotionally healthy childhood. But kids are resilient. If we think about our own childhoods, most of us didn't just sail through without any conflict. We often say we got through the rough patches, but those of us who can say there was someone present supporting us when we needed it are now able to equate the bad times with growth.

This book cannot address all of the complicated factors in early bullying prevention. But it does focus on 10 major "strings" from this complicated, tangled ball that are within our ability to untangle, which means recognizing and correcting behaviors from young ages, teaching communication skills, advocating in effective ways, supporting other parents, and laying the groundwork for raising responsible, digitally cool and kind citizens.

Paying attention to these basics will help our kids get what they deserve: our love and attention, and our best efforts to provide a safe and happy childhood with the potential for a confident adulthood.

Like untying any difficult knot, you start at the end, and trace its roots until you are finally able to undo the confusing, balled mess. Once you do, you are free to discover something whole and beautiful.

The Tangled Ball® Award is within your reach.

Susan S. Raisch
New York, Winter 2017

STRING TEN

From Sandbox to Safety Net

"Life is just one big adjustment."

These wise words from my mother-in-law, Mary Lee, were not shared to scare me but to prepare me. Instead of a negative, it became a positive way to highlight the importance of building a strong foundation as preparation for the unpredictable.

One of the basic building blocks in raising children is protecting and nurturing their spirit. It's like an engine. With help from us mechanics, it goes along at a good speed toward reaching its desired destination. As parents, teachers, coaches, and mentors, we help by keeping our foot gently on the gas by making education available, encouraging character (offline and on), and promoting interests and competence.

What happens to that engine when someone without our permission randomly throws a wrench under the hood or snaps a wire? It comes to a stop, or at best it sputters along but not at the same speed and certainly not at its full potential. Sometimes, in frustration, it will try to block the road for others.

Taking ownership of our role as their first teacher and advocate in their evolving stages of development is the first step in helping them get back on the road.

Social and Emotional Skills:
What to Expect at Different Ages

According to Understood.org, kids mature and develop at different rates, but there are social and emotional milestones you can expect at different ages. Keeping track of your child's progress as these skills develop can help reveal potential issues. The following timeline shows what's considered typical behavior as a child develops.

Ages 3 and 4

- Show and verbalize a wider range of emotion
- Show an interest in pretend play
- Show spontaneous kindness and caring
- Play with other kids, and separate from you more easily
- May still have tantrums because of changes in routine or not getting what they want

Ages 5 and 6

- Display awareness of their gender and may prefer to play with same-sex peers
- Enjoy playing with other kids and are more conversational and independent
- Test boundaries but are still eager to please and help out
- Begin to understand what it means to feel embarrassed

Ages 7 and 8

- Show more awareness of others' perceptions
- May complain about friendships and other kids' reactions
- Want to behave well, but aren't as attentive to your directions
- Try to express feelings with words, but may resort to aggression when upset

Ages 9 and 10

- Start narrowing peer groups to a few close friends they share secrets and jokes with
- May withdraw from family activities and conversations, and develop their own identity
- Are affectionate, silly, and curious, but can also be selfish, rude, and argumentative

What We Can Learn from Maryann and Scott

My neighborhood is fortunately connected by a series of sidewalks and porches. One day, six years ago, I was at the right place at the right time. A mother started telling me how upset she was that her pleasant, happy second grader was now moody, constantly tired, not doing as well in school and disinterested in the things he used to enjoy. The family is Catholic and her little boy was about to make his First Holy Communion, usually an exciting time but not for him. He just wanted to stay at home.

"You're only as happy as your unhappiest child," the saying goes, so needless to say, Maryann was miserable.

The next time I saw her was on the same sidewalk the following October. They were on their way back from his basketball game. Her body language had changed and her son, Scott, was running, laughing and having fun. When I asked him if his team won the game, he had a big smile and said lightheartedly, "We lost!" The loss aside, he was a happy camper.

Maryann gave me the update. Following a very difficult second grade year, and after trying to work with the teacher and principal, she and her husband made the decision to switch Scott to another class when the new school year started.

Although difficult at first, the change of classroom seemed to be working and third grade started off on the right foot.

Get Out Your Cape—You're on Duty!

During that time, Maryann was the expert. She looked under the hood and started to figure out why her son was stalled. Apparently, a boy in his class was systematically putting him down and Scott started to believe all the bad things being said about him. Since it was a small school and the same students stayed together year after year, Scott's parents felt forced to ask for a change of classroom.

Maryann was getting the distinct impression that the administration thought that she was a helicopter mom. However, Maryann and her husband had not exhibited a pattern of taking over their child's education and outside activities. They let the teachers teach and the coaches coach.

So how was she supposed to convince a group of professionals to help her when they had decided that she was the problem?

(I can't actually blame schools, though, for not wanting to enable overprotective parents who do get too involved in their child's school life. When a controlling parent does behave inappropriately, it's hard for teachers and administrators to do their jobs.)

Since Scott was only seven, the principal and the teacher were concerned that this wouldn't be the only time that Scott would run into problems, and they didn't think it was in his best interest to move classes at such an early age. In the end, though, they did agree to the change.

In a perfect world, the school would get to the core of the issue with the child causing the angst. It was also important for Maryann and her husband to continue teaching their son skills on how to handle tough social situations but some issues require intervention.

Red Alert: Perspective Needed ASAP

Maryann did many smart things when it came to her son, but one of them was "taking oxygen" first by talking to trusted people. She knew that she would be no help to him unless she first took care of herself. That's not much different than what we are told on an airplane, as part of the safety announcements for passengers traveling with young children. In the event of an emergency, we are told to take oxygen first for ourselves before placing an oxygen mask on our child.

Maryann needed to get perspective before she could work through the next steps she needed to take on behalf of her son. I felt privileged that she shared her dilemma with me. And she was right: If we don't keep our heads on straight, we can't be of any help to anyone else, even our own children.

Dealing with school-based issues can be very emotional. Schools, in general, are emotional places. I know one mom who actually meditates before she communicates with her child's teacher or the administration. It keeps her calm and focused. Meditation is not everyone's thing but taking a few deep breaths is never a bad idea. Our strong emotions are totally understandable but sometimes they don't help.

I was recently buying cold cuts at the neighborhood Italian deli and happened to be on line (the original and literal version: on a line) with Maryann. Scott is now 13 and still happy. His second grade tormentor has become a teammate and friend.

The story of Scott and Maryann shows us that kids can grow up just fine if we're patient and don't place negative labels on them. Relationships change as children do and sometimes for the better, especially if we keep our wits about us.

Whether you realize it or not, you are a role model for your children, and if you keep your cool and demonstrate some perspective, chances are your child will, too. So hike up your mom jeans and get behind the wheel.

Strengthening the Foundation of Their Expanding Worlds

According to Stan Davis, co-researcher of the *Youth Voice Project: Student Insights into Bullying and Peer Mistreatment* (a valued resource shared throughout the book), "Parents and guardians can help bullied and otherwise mistreated young people by spending time with them, by listening to them, by helping them build positive peer connections, by checking back with them over time, and by advocating for them at school."

The power of the Go-To Adult cannot be underestimated. It can be the difference between children internalizing the emotional pain caused by peer-to-peer abuse or overcoming a bump in the road.

In my own experience, I've been happy when one of my kids has opened up to me, but sometimes they've chosen someone else. In certain cases, children simply feel more comfortable talking with a teacher, counselor, grandparent, or family friend.

For a parent, it's hard to accept that when it comes to dealing with a particular issue, you're not "The One." Although it can be humbling, be proud that you've raised a child who has good instincts and knows how to communicate and solve problems.

As for those other trusted adults in our children's lives, they deserve our thanks.

Preparing to Parent in the Online Neighborhood

Experiences—good and bad—over the years make us somewhat "experts." As adults, when we tap into the trials and tribulations of life, we can truly help kids navigate with dignity and, hopefully, a sense of humor and wonder, especially now that we have a "new neighborhood." Perhaps not today, but chances are that soon enough they will be navigating the world of social media. Like every neighborhood, there's good and there's bad. Without a doubt, it's tricky, but not impossible to raise leaders offline and online.

Personally, I've had my share of embarrassing moments but thanks to the kindness of strangers, I got through them. Times, that if placed on any social media platform, I would go into hiding and wait for the world to end—like the day I wore my purple dress with the huge skirt to work. While working in mid-town Manhattan at Sesame Street (now Sesame Workshop), I stopped in the ladies' room before going down to grab some lunch at a deli next door. The shop was a popular spot, and as usual, it was bustling. Unfortunately, it wasn't the only thing bustling.

I had accidentally tucked the skirt into the back of my pantyhose. Uh huh, a woman's worst nightmare. Still unaware that anything was wrong, I went blissfully to the cash register to pay for my food. The woman cashier moved quickly around the counter and in one swift move, pulled my skirt back into place. I often think about her and hope she won the lottery. I am thankful that my embarrassment was contained to that deli and not serving as fodder for Instagram, Facebook, or Twitter.

Although I'm actually a fan of social media when it serves to connect people, I'm acutely aware of how vulnerable our kids are now. My hope, though, is that we can raise people who treat others with respect and kindness whether they're behind a screen or there in person, just like the cashier who saved me from further mortification.

In case you were wondering, I have not worn pantyhose since.

Tangled Ball® Worksheet

Every day, through interaction with their kids, parents try to establish a strong foundation for their children's future years. During the course of their busy lives, parents have little time to reflect. Take a few minutes now to think about what you consider to be the most important basics in preparing your children for living in a hyper-social world.

Q: "Life is one big adjustment." True? How do we help ourselves and our children accept change? Can this be a positive thing?

_____
_____

Q: Protecting the confidence and spirit of children is one of the key building blocks. What would you consider key components to a good social, emotional foundation for your school-aged children?

_____
_____

Q: What does "taking oxygen first" mean to you?

_____
_____

Q: How do we take ownership of our role as our children's first teacher and advocate?

_____
_____

Q: Compared to what life was like when you were growing up, what has changed? How do these changes affect how you parent?

_____
_____

STRING NINE

STRING NINE

Choosing to Pay Attention

"If parents believe in their children," says Rick Ackerly, author of *The Genius in Every Child: Encouraging Character, Curiosity and Creativity in Children*, "the children can overcome most obstacles."

This belief can begin only when parents pay attention to their kids and encourage resilience. The good news is, those skills can be taught. Handling uncertainty and problem solving are everyday challenges, which need our attention.

Remember the helicopter mom? We don't do our children any favors by not allowing them to make mistakes or figure things out on their own. Modeling resilience means surrounding them with supportive people, encouraging them to manage their emotions, and helping them come up with their own solutions for new situations. When we do these things on a consistent basis we are helping them build confidence. They will learn to trust that they won't fall apart when they come across unexpected behavior from others. Although we need to be available to advocate for them when necessary, they must also learn to stand up for themselves.

Parenting is an Art ... Not a Science

This book does not rely on data. When your child is being bullied, all the statistics in the world will not make a bit of difference in how he or she feels about it or how you will choose to respond. Whether bullying is on the rise or in slight decline is not the point. Children who are on the receiving end of mean behavior—or who get in trouble for not knowing how to act, or witness it and don't know what to do—don't care about statistics.

Let's leave statistics to the policymakers. Parenting is not a science ruled by numbers. It concerns your child or your neighbor's child or the ones you coach or teach. Active parenting—and becoming a superhero when needed—means helping children we care about to care for others and themselves.

Bullying is not the real enemy.

What we must really pay attention to is the self-doubt and sense of aloneness that bullying causes.

No child should feel alone because each of us has the power to be a Go-To Adult.

Scary and Hopeful

Research into bullying reveals both scary and hopeful information, which while bringing all of us a step closer to understanding the issue, can also guide us toward concrete ways to help.

Here's the scary stuff: More than 67 percent of students believe that schools respond poorly to bullying, with a high percentage of students believing that adult help is infrequent and ineffective.[2] In other words, by the time they reach middle and high school, most kids being harassed are trying to handle abusive behavior on their own. When kids feel isolated for long periods of time, bad things can happen. They can easily lose their confidence and begin internalizing negative messages about themselves.

Although this statistic is unsettling, it presents a challenge that can be met from a young age, specifically

---

[2] *Bullying: Facts for Schools and Parents,* Cohn, Andrea, and Andrea Canter, PhD, NASP Fact Sheet.

by teaching and encouraging communication skills. This news is encouraging and supports the importance of parental figures taking an active role in monitoring their young children's interactions. It also reminds us of the need for superheroes in mom jeans.

Here's the hopeful part: According to the Youth Voice Project, 47 percent of students surveyed reported that the most effective adult action is *listening,* while 56 percent reported that the most effective peer action was *spending time with me.*

According to Stan Davis and Charisse L. Nixon, PhD, of the Youth Voice Project (www.youthvoiceproject.com), bullied youth are most likely to report that actions accessing support from others make a positive difference.

It's our job as parents to provide whatever support we can and sometimes that means encouraging our own children to support their peers when bullying occurs. This could very well be an ongoing issue, as children mistreat each other on a regular basis. By acknowledging this fact, we can play a significant role in improving the lives of hundreds of thousands of kids simply by making it easier for them to do three things:

1. Reach out to adults.
2. Communicate effectively.
3. Support their peers in a positive and realistic way.

Stepping Up

During an appearance as a guest for a student-run assembly at a very diverse public elementary school in New York City, I was pleasantly surprised to see how children can stick up for each other. Appropriately enough, it was *Respect for All Week* and the school had incorporated *One Can Count,* an initiative I developed with author Kathryn Otoshi to reinforce the concept of children stepping up to help each other.

I was glowing as I observed a group of student leaders monitoring more than 400 of their schoolmates in a discussion on respect. Just as I was patting myself on the back for a job well done, I heard three fourth-grade boys behind me calling the student leaders names, like "Greasy Face," one I'd never heard before, which only shows that we should never underestimate the creativity of our children.

Part of me had to laugh at the irony, but as the insults escalated I wasn't sure whether I should call it to the attention of the principal sitting in front of me or say something to the kids myself. As it turned out, I didn't need to. One of the boys' fourth-grade classmates waited for the perfect moment to step up.

"Stop that," she said. "That's mean, and that will hurt their feelings."

The name-calling stopped immediately.

I wished I had a gold medal to place around the young girl's neck. I thought of a perfect quote in that moment from hockey legend Wayne Gretzky, but I doubted if the girl knew who he was and I didn't want to trivialize her actions.

"We miss 100 percent of the shots we don't take."

We don't live in a dream world like Camelot. Not every child has the personality or confidence to do what this little girl did, but many can learn how to step up in a variety of other ways when a moment of crisis occurs. I wonder if she knew at the time how critical her actions were and what she did to create a positive atmosphere in her school.

The principal and I were encouraged to see how one child can influence her peers with one well-timed, perfectly targeted statement.

Starting Young

Bullying awareness and prevention may have hit a peak several years ago, when we witnessed a rash of suicides by children as young as nine. The movie *Bully* was released, which put a face on peer-to-peer abuse. As these tragic events became public, the issue could no longer be ignored and the attention created a ripple effect, from the White House to newsrooms and from big cities to small towns.

As this shocking wave of suicides left the country breathless, experts and despondent parents wondered aloud how children could take their own lives.

Journalist Charles M. Blow wrote mournfully about watching these incidents and reflected on his own experience being bullied as an eight-year-old child.

"Children can't see their budding lives through the long lens of wisdom," he wrote, "the wisdom that benefits from years passed, hurdles overcome, strength summoned, resilience realized, selves discovered and accepted, hearts broken but mended and love experienced in the fullest, truest majesty that the word deserves. For them, the weight of ridicule and ostracism can feel crushing and without the possibility of reprieve. And, in that dark and lonely place, desperate and confused, they can make horrible decisions that can't be undone."[3]

Mr. Blow knew that bullying can be deadly, that it isn't a game, no matter how harmless some people may think it is, and that this fact must not be overlooked. He reminds us all that we must always remind our children—and ourselves—that words do matter, that they affect people in ways we often underestimate.

As more unthinkable events unfolded, pressure started to mount on school districts and politicians. As a result, more states began to put legislation into place requiring schools to have bullying prevention policies.

StopBullying.gov provides valuable information and updates on laws and policies by individual state.

They are not alone. Fortunately, many talented, intelligent, and creative organizations and individuals have developed well-researched programs and tools to prevent and combat bullying.

---

[3] Charles M. Blow, Op-Ed, *New York Times*, Oct. 14, 2011.

More training in these areas for parents and schools will certainly improve the negative statistics we still see. One of the most effective tools in the quest to improve the statistics is connecting the dots between available resources, schools, and homes.

A list of high-quality, research-based programs and initiatives are available on our website, TangledBall.com. Feel free to add your own favorites on the Tangled Ball® Facebook page.

It's up to each of us to wave our capes and make an impact in our homes and communities whenever we can. I suggest we emulate Maya Angelou and her call to action: "I did then what I knew how to do, now that I know better, I do better."

Tangled Ball® Worksheet

Our days are busy and there is much to do before bedtime. We can't fit in one more thing, can we? We can try. We can pay attention to how we can positively impact our children's ability to successfully navigate life. This means considering a few questions.

Q: Can resilience be taught? If so, how?

_____

_____

Q: In your opinion, does the issue of bullying get enough attention? If so, why? If not, why?

_____

_____

Q: Do parents have a responsibility to help schools respond effectively to students who feel they've been bullied? If so, what can parents do?

_____

_____

Q: According to the Youth Voice Project (YVP), the most effective adult action was "listening." Based on your own experience growing up, do you agree with this statistic?

_____

_____

Q: YVP reports that the most effective peer action was "spending time with me." Based on this statistic, how do we teach our children to be the "Go-To Kid?"

_____

_____

STRING EIGHT

STRING EIGHT

Keeping an Eye on the Prize

Not every child will experience real bullying in their early years, but most children will be on the receiving end of some mean behavior. As parents, our goal is to do what we can to reasonably ensure that any hard times for our kids will be just a brief chapter in their future memoir and not the whole book.

It doesn't take long before our kids learn that life is a mix of good and not so good. It takes a team effort from parents, teachers, and mentors to help them first identify bad behavior and then provide them with the resources to react accordingly without it becoming a chronic, internal problem.

The prize for achieving this is positive self-esteem, wholeness, security, and love.

Most of us will keep our eye on this prize, as we want our children to be stable and flourish. But this intention can often lead parents to feel pressure to be perfect and never make any mistakes, which is very difficult and perhaps unrealistic. This is especially true for parents dealing with bullying, particularly when there are no obvious, easy solutions, which is often the case.

"I think there's so much pressure on parents to be perfect, to do 'the right thing,' to always know the answers," says Cynthia Lowen, award-winning producer and writer of the documentary *Bully* and co-author of *The Essential Guide to Bullying: Prevention and Intervention*. "In thinking about my experiences with parents coping with bullying, often there are no clear solutions.

"Bullying is messy," she continues. "It affects the whole family, and every situation is completely unique. I think parents who can embrace their own vulnerabilities and open up the opportunity for creative problem-solving—and even humor—during incredibly tough times foster a sense of being in it together with their children. In seeing it through, the relationship will deepen and evolve."

Every battle cannot be won. Some situations will not go our way, but if a child develops a sense of perspective with the guidance of a Go-To Adult, confidence can grow.

Defining Goals

I loved my grammar school and felt blessed that everyone was nice to me. We had a classic mix of popular kids and nerds, and I felt like a part of every circle. Between 7th and 8th grade, my brave father of eight children announced to his surprised family that, due to a recession, we were about to embark on an adventure, which meant moving quickly from Indiana to Puerto Rico.

Looking back, it was a great experience—but at the time, I was devastated. My wonderful Midwestern grade school had been my safety zone and I cried every day, fearing what it would be like to leave it. I soon got a lesson in what it's like to be on the outside looking in and my empathy grew for kids who are considered unpopular and saddled with negative labels.

At a school reunion in Indiana 25 years later, I learned about the positive role one person can play by keeping their eye on the prize. It's a moment I hope I will never forget.

One by one, each of us at the dinner table stood up to give a little toast about our elementary school. I told everyone how much I had appreciated their collective support when I moved. Believe it or not, they had raised money to bring me back home so I could go on their 8th grade class trip to Washington, D.C.

My tribute was followed by many funny stories from people who remain each other's best friends to this day.

Then came Louis. He was one of the nicest kids in our class and like most of us, was a bit awkward. It didn't help that his mom, Mrs. Chapman, was also our fourth grade teacher. It had been painfully obvious to all of us at the time that he struggled as a student. Today, he would have been diagnosed with a learning disability. His mom was steady, though. She never gave him preferential treatment or became visibly annoyed when he had trouble keeping up. I was always amazed at that.

When it was his turn, Louis stood and spoke with eloquence about his mother's grace and love during those years, particularly in fourth grade. Most of us around the table cried, including some of the men. Although he had never let on during those elementary school years, Louis explained the pain of feeling different but how his mother made him feel valued.

"She never put me down."

Louis become an emergency responder and married a woman he cared for deeply. They went through extreme trials and tribulations, including when his wife became ill, but his mother's kindness sustained him and he always chose gratitude over resentment. He became his best self.

Language Matters

Luckily, Louis wasn't labeled because the words we use to describe children, such as *bully* or *victim*, often create a slippery slope. If they hear these words enough, they may decide that that's who they are, not how they're acting.

There is a big difference, which we must acknowledge. That's because while it's difficult to change a label, it's much easier to change a behavior.

Children need our attention whether they are being mistreated or are the ones doing the mistreating. The roles they occupy—bully, victim, target, and bystander—are roles they are playing and should not be used as labels. In other words, sometimes kids *act* like a bully; sometimes they're on the receiving end of that behavior; and most often they are somewhere in the middle, witnessing the hurtful behavior.

The language we choose to use in these cases can become crucial in how our children learn to cope with this behavior.

Mean or Bully?

I prefer using the word *mean* over *bully*, especially with young kids. For them, bully conjures up strong images, like Sid in *Toy Story*, the neighbor who goes around breaking things on purpose. He is a perfect example of someone we'd like to avoid.

When I've asked kids in younger grades if they're a *bully*, they look bewildered. They don't feel like they look or act like a Sid. In my interactions, they seem to understand the word *mean* and its implications.

Consider this chain: Mean equals Bad, which can be Horrible, especially when the Mean behavior becomes unrelenting, which makes kids feel Horrible and Alone, which leads to Sadness, which steals Confidence, and if unchecked, leads to Serious Unhealthy Behavior.

While much of what our children experience is not under our control, mean behavior happens, especially when they leave the nest and begin a pre-school program, and in spite of our efforts to protect them. Mean behavior is nothing new and it's not going anywhere.

But we can control what happens once we know about the mean behavior. Our children do not have to feel alone, and what begins as mean behavior does not have to progress to something seriously unhealthy.

So it's important what language we use to identify both parties, as this will go a long way in determining the mindset of all the participants, including you.

So is the child being bullied a target or a victim?

Victim is a rather permanent, negative, and powerless label. Target is a temporary role that has the potential to allow growth and positive change.

What do we call the child doing the bullying, a bully or a meanie? This may depend on the age of the children, and what words they already know to describe this behavior. In any case, it's important to label the action and not the person.

What about the children in the middle? Are they bystanders or *upstanders*?

A bystander is someone who actively or passively does not respond to someone who is hurting or being hurt—socially, emotionally, intellectually, and/or physically. An upstander, a term used by, among others, the National School Climate Center—an organization supporting safe, supportive school environments to improve learning—is an active role that targets a solution and not the problem.

Plato got it right a long time ago when he said, "Silence gives consent."

Throughout this book, *bully* and *target* will be used to describe behavioral roles. The word *victim* will not be used and *upstander* will be supported with enthusiasm.

We're Not All Mrs. Chapman

Not all parents are alike. Sometimes, we don't want to expose our children's perceived weaknesses or even our own. It's hard to trust others when we're feeling vulnerable. This results in a wildly divergent assortment of parenting styles, especially when it comes to handling conflict. In those cases, our strategy—if we even have one—is usually based on our individual experience and unique personality. Some parents have the ability to remain objective, but many of us tend to react in one of the following ways:

1. Protect
2. Retaliate
3. Ignore
4. Blame
5. Deny

Sound familiar? Let's examine each of these impulses and see where we can expand our options for reactive behavior.

#1: Protect

"I'm going to make sure no one is mean to my child."

We've heard that a million times, and I wish it were possible. Wouldn't it be nice if we had a special spray we could squirt them with before they went to school each day?

Some kids breeze through life with no social problems. If you have more than one child, they may be different when it comes to how they fare in the sandbox or in the classroom. Kids born with high social and emotional intelligence know how to navigate mean waters, but many kids—probably most—need some work in this area. So as a parent of a young child, be prepared for your kids to encounter some social challenges.

One of the best "teachers" I had was a third grader named Paul. Unlike many kids, he shared with his parents that he was being picked on by a group of classmates. When they offered to talk to the principal, he panicked. He nervously told them that if they did, things would just get worse. After getting to know Paul's class through my outreach involvement in his school, he was perfectly correct. He was the expert.

Paul is now in high school and is doing great, but it was a process. He was made to feel like a loser for many of the first years of school. But he is very bright, which seemed to be part of the problem as well as the solution. Although confused about why he was constantly put down, Paul was also smart enough to know that he was in a situation in which he didn't have the power.

This shows how a child can get stuck on a word. Loser is such a bad one.

There are no losers. There are just losing situations.

Paul's parents were careful, but they did address it with the school and kept a close eye on the situation. They made sure his education was satisfying his academic interests. He was also a good swimmer so they signed him up for a team outside of school, where he felt important because of his contribution to his team's success.

What can we learn from Paul's experience? First, he showed great resilience. Second, his parents kept his feeling of safety intact by being careful how they handled it with the school. They were able to support him by making sure he had other things to do and by correcting him whenever he drifted into the "if you can't beat 'em, join 'em" club.

If sports are not attractive to your child, try pets, music, theatre, arts and crafts, reading, Legos, chess, cooking, baking, bike riding, or even charity. Any of these offer possibilities for great satisfaction and personal growth.

When kids love spending their free time playing video games, it takes establishing limits and a bit of creativity to get them up and out. Through its website, HealthyChildren.org, the American Academy of Pediatrics offers a Family Media Plan for free download because screen time should not totally take the place of physical activity.

#2: Retaliate

"Just punch 'em back."

When others diminish our children it can inspire real anger. While I would describe myself as a "peace at any price" person, I have to admit to silently wishing ill will on children (and their parents) who I felt were making mine miserable, even if temporarily. I know that's weak and didn't help anyone, but we're all human.

I once witnessed a good friend of mine, a dutiful father with a tough streak of his own, grow tired of his 11-year-old son getting shoved around at school. He told Jake to "come out swinging" next time he was harassed. So when a boy in his class gave him a little shove in the stairwell, Jake whipped around, knocked him into the wall, and took care of business. His aggressor was stunned. Of course, the two were hauled into the principal's office. Jake got suspended and he missed his elementary school's graduation trip and big dance.

Did the bully back down? Absolutely. Did Jake miss out? Yes, he did. And the boy who was the original aggressor got to go on the trip.

My friend's retaliation plan had a 50 percent success rate. Most parents want their children to have happy memories of childhood. Whether it's realistic or not, we're always working toward a 100 percent success rate, but sometimes the choices we make cause some serious setbacks.

When it comes to kids we care about, it's a tough call. I heard recently about a principal who gave permission to—and encouraged—a fifth-grade boy to retaliate the next time his aggressor bothered him. At recess the next day, Daniel created the opportunity by letting a ball roll into this aggressor's territory, knowing that it would set up a reaction. The plan worked. The boy shoved Daniel, who immediately pushed him back against the side of a brick wall. Did the boy ever bother Daniel again? No. Were there any downsides? Yes. Daniel's Mom was upset for two reasons.

The boy narrowly missed having a serious injury and using your fist was not the message she and her husband were promoting at home. Also, many kids may not feel comfortable fighting back, which is why they may be targets in the first place. The principal showed support, but suggesting a physical response like that can backfire.

#3: Ignore

"It's no big deal. Kids will be kids. There will always be teasing. It's part of growing up."

If I had a nickel for every time I've heard this, I'd have a healthy retirement fund. There is truth to each of these claims, but only to a point.

I'm in the camp that believes that kids have to experience conflict. We can't expect them to be nice all the time. After all, look at us! They have to learn how to manage the challenges of other people's personalities and behaviors. Even typically good kids have a bad day or need to test their power. That's how they learn.

When encountering questionable behavior, parents often wonder if their child has entered "The Gray Zone," a fuzzy place where it's hard to tell if kids are being kids or if the situation requires some sort of intervention.

Get out your capes, but don't don them just yet.

Consider these two scenarios:

1. A child comes out of school crying because two other girls she's friendly with had a play date the day before and she wasn't included.

Question: Is this a big deal?

Answer: Probably not, but maybe. It's upsetting for her but perhaps not damaging—unless it's a pattern of direct meanness. Are the other girls making sure she knows she wasn't included? Did they leave her out on purpose?

2. A child comes home from school each day for an entire week, feeling diminished, because every time he goes into the bathroom, it's with a few boys at a time and one of them is always calling him names, causing trouble and making him feel uncomfortable. This happens only in the bathroom, where there's no teacher around.

Question: Is this a big deal?

Answer: Yes, because it makes the child feel unsafe. If the parent becomes aware of this situation, it should be addressed with the school and resolved.

Some elementary school administrators say that one of

their biggest challenges is that parents and students now consider everything as bullying—from being bumped in the hallway to being left out of a birthday party. These situations may be annoying, rude, or disappointing, but they are not necessarily serious or damaging.

One principal expressed his frustration about a handful of parents who would habitually descend upon the office, giving the school secretary a hard time, and demanding to talk to him because they felt their nine-year-old children were being bullied. (The irony of the parents' behavior did not escape him.) It turned out that there was some aggressive behavior going on, but the main problem was being caused by the virtual, interactive, violent video games the parents were allowing their kids to play at home.

Apparently, the boys were berating each other through headphones as each one sat alone in their living rooms, or worse, in the privacy of their bedrooms.

Online safety rule #1: Keep computers or game units in a public space at home.[4] Children need to feel safe but must also learn how to handle their emotions in an age-appropriate way. Giving young kids free reign with games that are labeled *Mature Audiences Only* may not be the best choice. Kids need to feel powerful and part of something, but simple common sense means we can find things for them that are cool, positive, and better for this early stage in life.

So while some bad behavior may seem benign, we must recognize that families impacted by legitimate, hurtful, and abusive behavior do not think that federal policy or local schools have gone far enough to address this type of cruelty. Although all 50 states have some type of bullying prevention law or policies, it is not clear whether they are effective or being properly enforced.

In any case, the need to genuinely support kids hasn't

---

[4] Source: CommonSenseMedia.org.

changed, which means that when a child is being taunted, it *is* a big deal and should not be ignored or dismissed as "kids being kids." Laws or no laws, most experts agree that an estimated hundreds of thousands of kids on any given day miss school because they fear mistreatment by their peers. As a nation of Go-To Adults, we can't let them down.

#4: Blame

"Why did you ...?"

No one wants to feel as if his or her child is a target. For parents, this can trigger a range of emotions, including embarrassment, anger (at the perpetrator), and in some cases, deep frustration with our own child for being a magnet for meanness. For example, it can be exhausting to keep coaxing a child to avoid some behaviors that may be making them more vulnerable.

Case in point; Angie and Angie, a mother and daughter with the same name, but as different in personality as night and day. Mom is very conservative in dress, ideas, and mannerisms. Daughter Angie is not. Even as a child, she pushed the limits and her school constantly sent her home for style offenses, including multicolored hair, which she dyed herself in fifth grade. Quite surprisingly, Mom pleaded with the school to be more accepting of her daughter's creativity, that she was an artist, and her instincts, while needing to be channeled, should not be stifled. Somehow, mother and daughter made it through the ensuing years of school and college. Perhaps because the mother refused to be embarrassed by her daughter's unique qualities, the daughter became a thriving adult with a job in finance, still faithful to her own style and enjoying her creativity.

We humans are inherently social and want to feel connected, even those of us who sometimes act and think differently than the norm.

"A deep sense of love and belonging is an irreducible need of all people," says Brené Brown, PhD, LMSW, author, speaker, researcher, and professor at the University of

Houston Graduate College of Social Work. "We are biologically, cognitively, physically, and spiritually wired to love, to be loved, and to belong. When those needs are not met, we don't function as we were meant to. We break. We fall apart. We numb. We ache. We hurt others. We get sick."[5]

For parents of children with special needs, this can be especially challenging, and we will address some of those issues in String 4.

#5: Deny

"You'll get over it."

Sometimes, doing nothing is exactly the right thing. But conflict does not always disappear without some intervention. Busy parents may prefer to see an issue fade away on its own and sometimes we're lucky that it can play out without our involvement. But if a child is acting unusually, and it goes on for a few days, it's time to stop wishing it away and get to the bottom of the problem.

Vittoria was in seventh grade when I met her. She had transferred the year before from a neighboring school and things were not going well. We happened to be sitting together in the hallway one day when I asked her how school was going. She just shook her head and had a soulful look. When I asked if she had friends, she just shook her head again. Then, in her soft-spoken voice, she said the boys would not stop teasing her and she didn't know why. I didn't, either. From what I could tell, there was nothing obvious to pick on. She just had the bad fortune of transferring into a class with cliques.

Since I was doing a volunteer project for six weeks, I chose Vittoria as my assistant. Many girls liked volunteering so I brought them together during recess to make signs and decorate hallways. It always pained me when I saw the subtle behavior among the girls that must have hurt as

---

[5] Interview with Emma M. Seppälä, PhD, *Psychology Today* (2012; online).

deeply as the overt teasing of the boys. When I gathered the girls into a circle one day, they would not make room for Vittoria. Even when I manipulated the seating arrangement, the girls that were always considered nice would not make eye contact with her. Even one of the nicer girls made a point of avoiding her. I wondered how Vittoria got up each day and came to school. I doubted if I could have done it.

Then I met Vittoria's mother. Beyond her lovely Italian accent, I noticed that she had a firm grasp of the problem, which obviously frustrated her, but she was steadfastly loyal to her daughter. By the time I met her, the problems were not new, but she wasn't giving up. Vittoria's mom did all the right things on the experts' checklists. She spoke to the teacher, wrote a note to the principal, and scheduled a follow-up meeting.

She was extremely realistic. She knew that her child would always feel like an outsider because the school had not made any effort to welcome new students. Vittoria had no one to team up with to eat lunch or share homework, so that left her alone to fend for herself.

While Vittoria obviously experienced the worst of being excluded, her mother remained nervous about the situation, especially how it might affect her future. Would it destroy her confidence? Would she ever have friends again? She felt a little guilty, as she had never thought that moving only a few miles away would change things so drastically.

But in front of her daughter, Vittoria's mom concentrated solely on validating her child's feelings. As a short-term help, she enrolled her at a dance studio where she made new friends. She also took a long-term view and guided Vittoria to a new and healthier situation in middle school and beyond.

Vittoria's story is a good example of what can happen when a parent does not deny what is happening, is steady, and works in partnership with the school. Slowly but surely the school mentored Vittoria *and* the girls who were guilty of the bad behavior. That's because both parties, including the girls who were acting badly, deserve unconditional attention, especially during this vulnerable stage of growth.

Childhood psychology experts agree that if bullying behavior in kids goes unchecked throughout their childhood and teen years, they are more likely to have problems in adult life where their behavior will not be monitored the same way.

According to a 2015 report from the Centers for Disease Control, "Students who engage in bullying behavior are at increased risk for academic problems, substance use, and violent behavior later in adolescence and adulthood."

Years later, after a good run through high school and college, I asked Vittoria how she had gotten through that tough time. She answered me with two words and a smile.

"My mom."

Her mom listened to her. As a result, Vittoria always felt that her mother was her advocate but she was never embarrassed by her subtle involvement with teachers or principals. Vittoria's mom respected her daughter's wishes.

Protect. Retaliate. Ignore. Blame. Deny.

These approaches have one thing in common: They don't necessarily take into account our children's long-term needs. If our desired goal as parents is to help our children feel good about themselves as they grow, then these challenges may require more strategy, listening, cheerleading, and patience.

Tangled Ball® Worksheet

"The days are long, but the years are short." This is true, of course, but it's hard to believe, especially when you're up in the middle of the night for a sick child, or the dog really does eat Johnny's homework, or your child is crying because her friend didn't include her for a sleepover. But these hectic times are the moments when our coping skills and our attention may impact our children as they grow up.

Q: What does "keeping your eye on the prize" mean to you?

_____

_____

Q: Kids tease each other. This is old news and it's no big deal. Do you agree? Why or why not?

_____

_____

Q: Are the words bully and mean interchangeable? Do you agree that language and avoiding labels are important?

_____

_____

Q: Protect. Retaliate. Ignore. Blame. Deny. These are the reactions parents often have when dealing with peer mistreatment. Do you identify with any of these approaches?

_____

_____

Q: What responsibility do we have for other parents and children coping with bullying?

_____

_____

STRING SEVEN

STRING SEVEN

Preparing for a New Neighborhood

When is your child ready to cross the street without holding your hand? How do you know when it's time to have them do it alone?

Safety is always our first concern, and just as it dictates our decision-making out of doors it should also be our primary criteria when deciding when to allow our kids to begin navigating the world of online communications. Just the thought of it is enough to send a chill up the spine of many parents.

Some may be wholly unprepared for what they are about to encounter. I recently met a woman who kept referring to Facebook as Faceoff. I was trying not to laugh, but I didn't correct her, either. Something in her slip-up struck me as oddly accurate because this still relatively new neighborhood can be awesome or just plain treacherous.

Once again, it's up to you. When is your child ready for a little independence? And when is it time to have your first "stranger danger" talk? Let's not even consider talking with our kids about sex or drugs and alcohol. We can save that for another book. What's crucial right now is figuring out when your child is ready to go online—supervised or not—and when it's appropriate to provide a cell phone for independent use.

Raising Responsible Digital Citizens

Most experts advise addressing big issues with your children before their peers become their primary source of influence. Deciding when and how to prepare for these moments are proactive decisions that parents who prepare will never regret.

"Parents often ask me what age determines when their kids are ready for a cell phone or to use social media," says Dr. Patricia Agatston, co-author of *Cyberbullying: Bullying in the Digital Age* and president of the International Bullying Prevention Association. "My response to them is, When are *you* ready? When are *you* ready to brush up on the digital world that kids are inhabiting and when are *you* ready to have these crucial conversations about both the opportunities and responsibilities of digital citizens?"

When my kids get together, their favorite comedy routine is imitating the way I first introduced the "sex talk." I thought I did a great job, but I've eventually come to find out that they thought it was hysterical. I also learned that by the time I approached my youngest, he had already asked his older sister some of the questions he should have asked me. Kids were talking about it at a much younger age by then and I didn't realize it.

Luckily, my oldest daughter became the Go-To Adult, which was very much appreciated. After all, it could have been my son's peers, who were definitely not the best source.

While you may be unwittingly providing good material for your kids' future stand-up routines, it does require courage and steady nerves to talk to your kids about tough topics. They may roll their eyes, but that's why good Go-To Adults are superheroes in my mind and should get medals of honor. If not you, then who? Whether kids admit it or not, they count on adults to be in charge, which is good, especially when it comes to delicate subjects because, as we all know, if no one is steering the bus, it may go off the road and the wheels may eventually fall off.

How many sad celebrity tales are out there about child stars who didn't have solid mentoring while growing up and never really got it together as functioning adults? Their wheels fell off in public, which means their behavior was online for everyone to see, including, perhaps, your children.

While working on many high-quality outreach campaigns spearheaded by television networks and others, I spent countless hours in strategy sessions discussing issues ranging from literacy to health to teen obesity and juvenile justice. Inevitably, the subject of signing a celebrity teen spokesperson came up. I consistently advised against using star power from people that age because the risk was too high. The chances that these teens would eventually be in the news for bad behavior were greater than their odds of sustaining a good image. Possibly, they don't have skilled Go-To Adults in their lives so perhaps we shouldn't expect so much of them as role models for our children.

Training Wheels

Young children are especially impressionable and take lots for granted. That's why we never stop reminding them about the dangers of careless drivers, looking both ways before crossing the street, and knowing who they are communicating with online. There are easy-to-navigate sites created for younger children that can serve as training wheels for this new adventure.

Dr. Agatston, who is also a counselor with the Prevention/Intervention Center in Georgia, explains that social networking sites for younger users, such as Yoursphere and Club Penguin, are a great way to introduce safe social networking.

"The biggest challenge is that kids want to use it with other friends that they know," she says. "So your child may need to convince a few of her friends to use it as well. Also be aware that social play sites, such as Club Penguin, offer limited free play compared to what paying members receive."

Luckily, many resources, including ConnectSafely.org and CommonSenseMedia.org, help parents make well-informed decisions about choosing a first mobile phone with texting abilities, seeing a PG movie, signing up for a social media site, or handling cyber-bullying.

"Waiting until middle school to address online safety issues and cell phone use is too late," says Krista Wright, a seventh-grade teacher at Lynnfield Middle School in Massachusetts. "I'd love to see parents start getting educated about these things as early as kindergarten."

Read the Fine Print

"Everybody in my class has Instagram!"

This may be true, but it's also a little sobering. Most sites have minimum age requirements ranging from 13 to 17.

The Facebook Terms of Services state that "You will not use Facebook if you are under 13." Why 13? It might not be what you think. This age barrier is about marketing as opposed to maturity. The Childhood Online Privacy Protection Act (COPPA), a federal law enforced by the Federal Trade Commission, prohibits websites and online services from collecting personal information, such as physical and email addresses, telephone numbers, photos, and geo-location information, from children under the age of 13 for marketing purposes without permission from their parents. When sites such as Facebook are not technically aimed at children, they comply with this rule by making 13 the minimum age as part of their Terms of Service. In other words, Facebook and other sites might not have protections in place to buffer kids from data tracking.

We all know how that's worked out. Many adults and children have chosen to ignore the Terms of Service. On Facebook alone, millions of children under the age of 10 have their own accounts. The same approach goes for

Instagram, SnapChat, Twitter, and other popular sites, apps, and games. Please remember that most of these attractions have been created by adults—for the enjoyment of other adults. Please consider carefully where you will allow your precious children to wander in this new neighborhood.

My mother used to say that if you get old enough, you start to understand everything, so I understand why some parents opt to say yes when their underage kids ask if they can have certain social media accounts. Some common justifications include:

> It's a way to stay connected with family.
> I don't want my kid to feel out of it.
> My older child has one, so it doesn't seem fair to
>   my younger child.
> This is how my shy child communicates.
> They just want to feel like part of a group.
> It's okay because I monitor it.

As the expert in your child's life, you decide risk versus reward, but that choice should be deliberate and not by default. Because kids want to feel connected, we must pay attention to what they are connecting to and think hard about how well we are capable of monitoring their internet travels.

Although there are products to help parents supervise their children's online activity, becoming a good digital citizen is more about maturity than technology and that happens only through ongoing guidance. Since the online world is fast and unpredictable, it's difficult to nurture empathy and social emotional intelligence.

My neighbor's daughter is 12 years old, and she recently started a Facebook page. She was happy to show me, but within a minute of logging on to her account Samantha began to squirm when she saw photos of her teacher taken in class by her classmates and posted with rude comments. Our tour became quickly uncomfortable. Samantha's mom was shocked and quite upset. Samantha was more annoyed than alarmed, probably because she was worried about losing access to this world she wanted to be a part of that had quickly become her new normal.

The Internet is *Not* Child's Play

Dr. Agatston suggests acquainting yourself well in the digital world before assuming that your child will safely navigate the unpredictable world of social media. She warns parents that sites like Instagram contain far more than cute photographs, and that they need to know that all is not so innocent on any of the sites designed for older people.

As an example, she tells the following story.

"A parent of a 5th grader was in a parent presentation I was giving and shared her experience with Instagram. She said that she allowed her daughter to download Instagram because all of her friends were using it and she didn't think there was much concern, since her daughter was only posting pictures of kittens and butterflies, all innocent stuff.

But she didn't understand about the privacy settings, and one day she noticed that her daughter had quite a large number of followers. While her daughter was only following a few friends, the fact that her mother and she didn't understand the privacy settings meant that she had left her account public and many unknown users were following her.

Her mother clicked on the followers and found several adult men who had very inappropriate images in their accounts. Her mother was mortified and deleted her daughter's account. Fortunately, her daughter had not accessed any of her unknown followers' accounts yet to view their pictures, but it was a good lesson in why parents need to understand and share with their children the importance of privacy settings."

Crossing the Digital Street in a New Neighborhood

Dr. Agatston has graciously allowed me to share several of her tips for parents entering the digital world with their children for the first time.

1. Begin by modeling a balanced use of technology. Kids are great observers (but sometimes poor interpreters) so make sure to put down the phone or other device during meals, traveling in the car, and having conversations with family and friends. Explain frequently why you are doing this in a way that communicates your value of being fully present with others.

2. Explain basic safety and identity theft prevention measures to your kids for being online. Examples include not sharing their home address, date of birth, and phone numbers; keeping passwords private; and posting only information that they are comfortable with everyone seeing.

3. Discuss the idea of a digital footprint and show them examples by doing a search on you or another family member's name that illustrates how much information can be found online. Explain that our digital footprint can be neutral, helpful, or harmful to us. Remind them that anything we share digitally can potentially become available for public viewing.

4. Discuss cell phone etiquette, both for the use of their own phone and using a friend's phone. Weave the concept of privacy into this conversation as well and why it's not appropriate to look through others' personal messages and photos without their permission, including that it's not okay to share personal communications with others. Ask your child to think about how he or she would feel if a personal communication to a friend were passed around to others without permission.

5. If there are certain sites or types of content that are off limits to your child, have a conversation about why that site is problematic and why certain content might be

harmful or against your personal values, morals, and ethics, rather than just banning the site.

6. Talk to your kids in a developmentally appropriate way about watching out for "tricky people" online who might try to get their personal information for identity theft or might be dishonest about their own identity. Explain that not everyone is who they appear to be online and that requests for photos from someone unknown to them should be refused. Give examples of how sometimes individuals pretend to be with modeling or acting agencies since that is appealing to many young people but it is rarely legitimate. Let them know they can always come to you if they receive such requests.

7. When you and your child are ready, start slowly to allow one social networking site and familiarizing yourself with the privacy settings and functions of the account. Connect Safely offers great guides for parents on social media sites in general and specific sites such as Instagram and Snapchat.

8. Set guidelines regarding the downloading or purchasing of apps. Consider if you want all app downloads to require your approval first. Common Sense Media has an app that will allow you to quickly look over the pros and cons of various apps and the recommended age guidelines.

9. Discuss how being a positive digital citizen affects others. Social networking sites and gaming sites rely on users to make the experience a positive one for everyone. That's why so many of these social sites allow users to flag inappropriate content and report cyber-bullying. Talk to your child about his responsibility to be an upstander when he sees cyber-bullying or other hurtful behavior. Explore together the various reporting functions of the sites your child uses, which allow users to report or flag problematic content. Discuss various scenarios that your child may witness and what strategies she can take to help another user.

More Rules of the Road

The first person I met at an online safety conference was Nancy Gifford. This online safety world was completely new to me and I felt like a 12-year-old kid at a new middle school attending the first dance by myself.

Okay, maybe it wasn't that bad, but I did feel a bit out of my element in that environment and slightly awkward. Luckily, it was Nancy's first conference, too, and we became fast friends.

At the time, Nancy had three young children and a law degree with an impressive career but she felt this issue deserved her attention. In the span of just a few years, Nancy had become an expert and someone I trust. Based on her parent experience as well as her work in the field, she had a few tips to share:

1. Google the popular social media sites and find out the minimum age requirement *before* your child asks to have an account. You may be surprised that the minimum ages can range from 13 all the way to 17.

2. Value honesty. It means the same thing online as it means offline.

3. Create a family computer/cell phone contract with your children so that you can create rules and repercussions together. There are lots of sample contracts online and you can use those to give you ideas for drafting your own.

4. Stick to the contract. If the rule is "You must pick up the phone or text back when I call or text you," and they don't, stick to the consequences in the contract.

5. Make sure they understand how they're coming across to you and to friends in their texting style. For example, when they're young, they may not understand that things like all caps can be interpreted as yelling.

6. Friends Unite. Decide as a group when your offspring will be allowed on sites such as Instagram or Snapchat or all the new ones being hatched every week. Back up each other on the rules and share information

about new sites or trends in what your kids may be seeing or how they're using social media, in general. We need each other.

Being True to Yourself

As mentioned, online safety is a little about technology and a lot about maturity. That's true for all media. Ronald G. Slaby, PhD, and Senior Scientist at the Center on Media and Child Health at the Children's Hospital Boston/Harvard Medical School, feels that parents need to help their children develop healthful media diets.

"The content and amount of media they consume will have important and lasting positive or negative effects on what they learn and how they behave toward others," he says. "Children who consume primarily educational media—where role models solve their social problems with acts of kindness, empathy, assertiveness, and respect—will learn to help others and cooperate. But children who consume primarily media violence, where violent behavior is typically glorified as being funny, justified, commonplace, exciting, rewarded, heroic, manly, effective, and/or pleasurable—will learn to treat each other in hurtful and violent ways."

I learned the value of this message many years ago when my second daughter, Molly, had to be hospitalized at the age of seven. As parents who have been through this know, it totally upends your life. I depended on the kindness of friends to keep our other three children, including Peter, who was then 11, busy. In all honesty, I wasn't even aware of what was happening at home.

A few weeks after Molly totally recovered and things went back to normal, I ran into my son's best friend's mom, Tina, in the grocery store. As we stood in the frozen food aisle, she recounted how during the hospital stay, she picked up Peter to go to the movies. When they got there he noticed that it was PG-13. He told her that he wasn't allowed to see it.

Despite where we were standing, I got warm in the face. What had I done to my son, and to this nice woman who was just trying to help? Because of my rules, she had been inconvenienced with four boys in her van, expecting to go to a cool movie.

Then I started dreading the possibility that Peter's friends may have given him a hard time for that. As it turned out, this woman thought my son was brave. The day worked out fine because she took the boys to a sports center and bought them pizza. They had a great time, and for that, I was relieved and grateful.

This wonderful mother taught me something that day about the importance of attitude and how it can set a positive tone. As she watched the boys run around outside instead of spending two hours nervously wondering whether they would be exposed to adult language and subject matter on her watch, a light bulb went off inside her.

Who needs conformity all the time? What a lesson. Stay the course.

As my daughter, Alice-Kate, likes to say:

"Be you... bravely."

STRING SEVEN

Tangled Ball® Worksheet

Who taught you how to use cell phones and social media? Thought so. Your generation was largely on your own. As pioneers, you may not have had mentors helping you navigate the intensity of new technology. Your children are lucky. They have you to help them reap the benefits and avoid the pitfalls. Yay you!

Q: Think back to when you were in elementary school. Fill in the blank: But everyone in my class has _____. How does that compare with what your own children want?

_____

_____

Q: Introducing online safety is a personal choice. How do you determine yours?

_____

_____

Q: What is digital citizenship?

_____

_____

Q: Based on age and/or maturity level, is it fair to make different rules for siblings?

_____

_____

Q: What online safety and digital citizenship advice would you give other parents?

_____

_____

STRING SIX

Big Leaders

Most of us want to be effective role models for our children and raise them to be leaders in one way or another. But what does leadership mean to you?

For some, it's personal. For example, in his current role as CEO of TVR Communications, Keith Washington says he values passion, humility, and loyalty. The father of three (including actress Kelly Washington of the movie *The Fat Boy Chronicles*), Keith explains, "I want to serve others with passion, I want to have bold ideas delivered with humility, and I want my team to be driven to win while staying loyal to their teammates."

So how do you fulfill the role of a leader? How does your child understand it? Does every child see herself as a potential leader? As they progress through their school years, certain students take leadership positions in the classroom or with a student council. Others need to be reminded that they can be leaders outside of these established systems; that running a student organization is not the only way to lead. We can help our children recognize their leadership abilities and appreciate the value of their unique potential.

Leadership means different things to different people, organizations and institutions. Words that define leadership and leadership traits vary in different settings. Here are some prominent ones from two environments:

In the Workplace

Accountable	Forward-Looking
Adaptable	Honesty
Aware	Inspirational
Commitment	Intelligent
Communication	Intuitive
Competent	Open-Minded
Confidence	Organized
Creative	Proactive
Optimistic	Quiet
Decisiveness	Respectful
Delegator	Self-Awareness
Empathetic	Self-Regulation
Focused	Succinct

Military Leadership Traits

Bearing	Integrity
Courage	Judgment
Decisiveness	Justice
Dependability	Knowledge
Endurance	Loyalty
Enthusiasm	Tact
Initiative	Unselfishness

Overcoming Barriers to Leadership

We depend on good leaders, whether they're running our country, businesses, school districts, classrooms, or homes. When there is a gap in leadership, we feel it. So do our children, so that's why it's vital we pay attention to our own actions and make sure we are being effective leaders in our own homes and communities.

Two barriers exist that can keep children from becoming leaders: staying to themselves and not interacting—or at the other end of the spectrum, being aggressive.

Quiet

"A quiet temperament is a hidden superpower."[6]

Of all the leadership traits listed earlier, "Quiet" may be the most surprising. Although extroverted people bring people together, quiet people are often the most effective managers because of their ability to observe and listen.

As a child, my daughter, Molly, was an introvert stuck living with a lot of extroverts. This gave us new perspective. For instance, *quiet* and *shy* are not always interchangeable. Quiet people are simply stimulated by more quiet activities. They are observers. Ironically, all through grade school Molly's nickname was "The President."

As an adult, she recommended two books by Susan Cain, called *Quiet: The Power of Introverts in a World That Can't Stop Talking* and *Quiet Power: The Secret Strengths of Introverts*. The companion website, Quiet Revolution (QuietRev.com), is great for the Go-To Parents of quiet and powerful children.

There are many myths about introversion. When I hear parents describe their quiet child as shy in front of them, I cringe a bit. Labeling a child keeps them in a box. When they are free of labels, they are free to evolve.

Aggressive

When a child exhibits a lot of anger, it has to be channeled. Early development professionals suggest trying to do this through positive activities, such as sports, art, music, meditation or volunteering. It's also suggested to limit what they watch on television or what video games they play. Getting to the bottom of the anger is key. It could be that they are on the receiving end of mean behavior themselves and don't know how to handle it. Or it could be that it's their nature and it has to be redirected. Either way, it's hard to constantly receive attention in the form of discipline.

---

[6] *Quiet Power: The Secret Strengths of Introverts* by Susan Cain, with Gregory Mone and Erica Moroz.

Aggressive children often lead in negative ways and take as much effort as a more reticent child to overcome some barriers. It takes a great deal of effort but once they learn to communicate their feelings in a healthy way and begin getting positive attention, their confidence and ability to see themselves differently will work in their favor.

According to the article, "Anger Management for Kids & Parents," posted online by The Child Development Institute, "Parents and teachers must allow children to feel all their feelings. Adult skills can then be directed toward showing children acceptable ways of expressing their feelings. Strong feelings cannot be denied, and angry outbursts should not always be viewed as a sign of serious problems; they should be recognized and treated with respect.

"To respond effectively to overly aggressive behavior in children we need to have some ideas about what may have triggered an outburst. Anger may be a defense to avoid painful feelings; it may be associated with failure, low self-esteem, and feelings of isolation; or it may be related to anxiety about situations over which the child has no control.

"Angry defiance may also be associated with feelings of dependency, and anger may be associated with sadness and depression. In childhood, anger and sadness are very close to one another, and it is important to remember that much of what an adult experiences as sadness is expressed by a child as anger." [7]

Assertive or Aggressive?

The difference between aggression and assertiveness is simple. One can get you in trouble. The other can get you what you want. The benefits of learning how to firmly, simply, and respectfully advocate for one's self are innumerable and lifelong.

---

[7] Adapted from "The Aggressive Child," Luleen S. Anderson, PhD, published by the Children's Bureau, ACYF, DHEW (ChildDevelopmentinfo.com)

Two-year-olds have no trouble saying no. Who knew that channeling the inner toddler could be so beneficial?

Promoting assertiveness means supporting the right to be heard, respected, and supported, which includes asking for help when needed. When we promote only aggression as a means of getting what you want, kids don't necessarily learn why they deserve to be treated well. Assertiveness requires a certain amount of self-esteem and also contributes to a positive sense of self.

It behooves us all to model these traits as best we can in our daily interactions. We'll be rocking our mom jeans and our invisible capes will be showing.

Assertiveness Tips from Experts and Friends

1. Explain the difference between aggressive and assertive. Aggressive behavior is bold, loud, or harsh and doesn't care about the other person's feelings. Assertive behavior is being clear about what you want and deserve. It is firm but it cares about the other person's feelings.

Assertive isn't always a reaction to a negative. It can be a way of communicating how we *want* to be treated. As my son, Jack, would say, "We hold the map on how we want others to treat us."

2. Reinforce reasons why kids should assert themselves in different situations. For example, you don't have to give part of your lunch every day to the pushy kid at your table, especially if you don't want to.

3. Support kids who try being assertive based on their individual personalities. For example, telling them to be bold when that's not in their nature will make them feel nervous. Too much criticism may also cause them to retreat. Their comfort zone is key.

4. Allow children to be assertive with siblings in the right situations. It can be intimidating and may cause temporary conflict, but it will boost their confidence when they are on their own. Of course, they need to respect their brother or sister in the process.

In general, siblings play a big role. Family therapist Louise Parente, PhD, LCSW, reminds us of the role siblings can play for each other when it comes to navigating effective behavior. She recommends that parents encourage communication at home between siblings, who more often than not, actually listen to each other. Parents can support this by creating safe spaces at home where children feel that they are working together, not alone or with outsiders, like other children, cell phones, computers, and TVs.

5. Especially with young children, give them words to use. For example, "That's my pencil. Please don't take it off my desk again."

6. Use role-play as a fun and effective way to make your points. This can include demonstrating what good body language looks like, making eye contact, and using direct language. Role-play is a great teaching tool and is mentioned several times in this book.

7. Compliment your kids when they get it right.

8. Keep expectations realistic. Parenting—and being a kid—is a work-in-progress for all of us.

Favorite Leadership Traits

What leadership traits do you value most? Children can easily model leadership qualities when a Go-To Adult nurtures any number of them. These traits may include honesty, integrity, courage, perseverance, or hard work, among others. As leadership teachers for our children, we can always improve our own skills.

The Tangled Ball® philosophy includes five essential tips for Go-To Adults:

- Practice What You Preach
- Stop Mean Behavior in Seconds
- Catch Kids in the Act of Doing Something Good (Upstanders!)
- Focus
- Everyone Needs Validation

Practice What You Preach: You've heard this before, but seriously, kids say and do *everything* you say and do.

My friend, Colleen, has a child who had a speech delay. Fortunately, the New York City school system provides speech therapy, but it's challenging. As her friends, we silently prayed that Jordan would eventually respond to the therapy and begin to communicate verbally. He eventually did.

The breakthrough occurred while sledding. After Colleen, her husband, and a teenager working on the slopes struggled to get Jordan situated safely in a snow tube, Jordan actually said three words in a row as he was launched down the hill.

"For **** sake!"

Colleen was horrified, as she was certain she was directly responsible as the role model for this language, but she was elated, too. Every time I think of it, I laugh. Jordan is living proof that even when you don't think a child is listening, he is, and he may blurt out your favorite words or phrases in a very public setting. This applies to what you say about anyone—teachers, neighbors, relatives, friends, or even a stranger in a store. Gossip is contagious and almost always unkind. Your kids are always learning, whether you want them to or not.

Stop Mean Behavior in Seconds: In order to teach children that a few words, a look, or a small gesture will stop a bullying action in seconds, we need to master the skill ourselves. That means being clear and direct, speaking in a low voice (kids tend to ignore screaming), and using one sentence or less to describe what they did wrong and how to correct it.

One afternoon, my husband and I observed our street filling up with kids under the age of 11, running from yard to yard playing sports or some other games. Conflict was inevitable but most of the time they handled it themselves. Emotions exploded over a game, which led to some physical conflict. Bats became involved but luckily no one got badly hurt. Each child, though, was sent home to talk to his parents.

My husband and I went into a long-winded litany of everything we thought we knew about parenting. After our diatribe, we overheard our neighbor talking to his son.

"There's right and there's wrong," he said. "That was wrong."

Bingo! That father hit it right on the money while we were delivering lengthy lectures no one would ever remember. And he nailed it wearing dad jeans, too.

Catch Kids in the Act of Doing Something Good: Make sure your child *accidentally* overhears you saying something nice about them.

That's some of the best parenting advice I've ever heard. In order for it to work, it has to be genuine, but what a confidence boost! It shouldn't be too hard to figure out when to do your thing, either, whether it's during a phone call when your kids are nearby but out of your eyesight, in the car while talking to your spouse, or when you're talking to your child's coach or dance teacher as they are packing up to go home. Your child may not want to let on that they heard you, but it will make them happy and even motivate them to get caught in the act of doing something good again.

Focus: Let's be realistic—focusing every ounce of attention on our kids 24/7 is impossible and arguably not healthy.

Before working remotely was common, MTV allowed me to have a home office, which saved me a three-hour commute each day, which at the time, with three small children at home, was a great situation, and I didn't want to mess it up.

One day, with a conference call scheduled for mid-afternoon, I ran into a jam because my usual babysitter was away. I juggled the best I could, but this meeting involved eight other people discussing something important, or so I thought at the time.

As soon as it was my turn to speak, my youngest toddler decided she needed my attention. With the phone to my ear, I crawled on my knees into the front closet. As I tried to outline my public relations strategy among the winter coats, snow boots, and fallen hangers, I heard this poor baby on the other side of the door scratching to get in.

Why is Mommy hiding in a closet?

Not a high point in my life as a parent. Needless to say, my daughter did not have my undivided attention and when the guilt became unbearable I told my colleagues I had to hang up. The client was not thrilled, but my daughter was pretty happy to have her mother back.

Sound familiar? I went to bed feeling I was a terrible mother and a not-so-professional professional. It was a wake-up call for learning to prioritize and understand my limits. Sometimes work or other responsibilities have to come first, but kids are little humans that need to feel important, which takes real planning.

Everyone Needs Validation: One day, while waiting for an important TV reporter to return a call, I watched as all the neighborhood kids, including mine, played in our yard after school. I put the oldest in charge when I heard the phone ring and lunged to pick it up on time.

Then I heard screeching. When I looked outside, I saw a three-tricycle pile-up. I was mortified. Even though he was on deadline, I had to tell the reporter I would call him back. When I did, I felt I had no other choice but to tell him the truth. He simply laughed and told me to hold on. All I could hear was a gaggle of loud kids arriving home from school. He was trying to pull off the same thing as me.

We bonded over this crazy journey of trying to raise kids while making enough money to feed and educate them.

It has also made me appreciate what it was like before cell phones ruled our existence. Being accessible all the time, especially when kids need our attention, takes discipline. I admire parents who create technology boundaries and know when to put their phone away. Not just down. Away.

For example, one parent I know asks everyone in the house, including visitors, to put their phones in a basket during mealtime.

Texting and Other Annoying Distractions

According to a 2015 survey, Americans check their phones eight billion times a day.[8]

While at my favorite coffee shop, I noticed a young mom having breakfast with her child, who appeared to be about four years old. The little girl seemed to be excited to have some special time with her mom.

As soon as they ordered, the mom was on her phone. Her little girl desperately tried to get her attention. First she was cute, pointing out things in the restaurant, bubbling over with enthusiasm. Then the food came, and the mother managed to eat without breaking focus on the phone. As the little girl picked at her meal her enthusiasm waned. Cute turned to sullen, which was sad to watch.

Of course, I don't know if this woman was texting something important or paying bills online or doing something productive, but it's quite possible that it was a habit, and mother and child missed out on a happy morning. I suppose it also could have been a newspaper, magazine or another distraction that kept her from paying attention to her daughter, but phones are a steady challenge to keep in place.

Texting is amazing, no doubt. It takes two seconds to tell someone if you're late, or decide on a meeting place or share a quick laugh. What did we do without them?

However, when a parent's texting is constant and

---

[8] Deloitte's 5th Mobile Global Survey.

chronic, the unintended message being sent to their children is that they are not as important as the person on the other end of the phone. This may be the "new normal" but it puts young kids at a disadvantage. They don't know how to ask you to put the phone down and pay attention.

Relationship Changer

These are unintentional teaching moments. Children follow in our footsteps, our text steps, and our social media steps. Becoming unaware of the people around us while being absorbed by a little screen is rude—plain and simple. It also takes away from building healthy interactions.

My husband calls the cell phone a relationship changer. It can either enrich our relationships with one another through positive communication, or it can be off-putting when one person is obsessively checking for messages, or writing texts, or answering a call at inappropriate times.

People who would never consider themselves rude in face-to-face situations can become thoughtless when it comes to cell phone habits. Deciding at what age your children should get a phone is a personal choice, but they have already learned by witnessing you what kind of phone habits they will take on as their own.

Redefining "Stepping Up" for Go-To Adults

As we explore what it means to be effective role models for our children, how do we demonstrate support when they come to us about mistreatment? Before we send our children to martial arts or tell them not to worry, it's important to hear directly from them.

According to the kids who participated in the Youth Voice Project, this is what helps and what doesn't:

Most Helpful Adult Actions

- Listened to me
- Gave me advice
- Checked in with me afterward to see if the behavior stopped
- Kept up increased adult supervision for some time

Least Helpful Adult Actions

- Ignored what was going on
- Told me that if I acted differently, this wouldn't happen to me
- Told me to solve the problem myself
- Told me to stop tattling

Tattling or Telling?

This is a big subject. Once again, there could be double messages with serious consequences. Naturally, there are good reasons we teach kids not to tattle. There's a big difference between a child trying to get someone in trouble versus a child needing to report something wrong. It's an important lesson and one that should be taught, but even when explained, most young children may not have the sophisticated analytical abilities to understand the distinction. The danger is that they may grow accustomed to not telling on someone for fear of being reprimanded or for fear that the adult doesn't want to hear it.

It takes patience, but in order for kids to keep telling us what's happening in their worlds, it's safer to listen to everything they say, and unless they are falsely accusing another child (which should have consequences), they should be taken seriously.

We can always come back with a positive response that either validates or corrects them.

For example, if one child reports that another child

hasn't followed a rule, the response can be, "It's good you know the rules." The child receives the attention they need but has not been encouraged to get their peer in trouble. As they grow and as we reinforce the differences between tattling and telling, they will eventually have the ability to understand why one is hurtful and the other helpful.

Modeling Leadership

When I asked a diverse group of third graders at St. Adalbert School on Staten Island, New York, about leadership, specifically who they would consider a leader, they listed the following:

Parents
Friends
Government
Mayor
Rosa Parks
George Washington
Abraham Lincoln
Cousins *
(*I can relate. I love my cousins, too.)

When I asked the students at Staten Island's P.S. 29 Bardwell School, they had a similar list, but one girl added international activist Malala Yousafzai from Pakistan, who through extraordinary personal sacrifice brought global attention to education for girls.

"We are all ordinary. We are all boring. We are all spectacular. We are all shy. We are all bold. We are all heroes. We are all helpless. It just depends on the day."[9]

---

[9] Brad Meltzer, father, *New York Times* bestselling author, TV host and creator of the illustrated children's book series *Ordinary People Change the World*.

Tangled Ball® Worksheet

We may not always think of parenting as a leadership position, but it is. Good leaders have expectations for the people they lead, even though in this case, the people are your offspring. Take a moment to consider your priorities and leadership style.

Q: What does leadership mean to you?

_____

_____

Q: If you had to write an honest list of your leadership strengths (without worrying about being egotistical), what would they be?

_____

_____

Q: Kids watch everything we do. Fill in the blank. "I would be so proud if my child follows my example by _____." Explain why you wrote what you did.

_____

_____

Q: Fill in the blank. "When I _____, I am teaching my child something that I didn't intend to teach." Explain.

_____

_____

Q: Do you agree with the list of "Most Helpful Adult Actions?" When you were a kid and had something troubling on your mind, what were some of the things that an adult did—or you wish they did—that made you feel better.

_____

_____

STRING FIVE

Little Leaders

Parenting is humbling. Just when we think we know all about it, our little children teach us another thing or two. For example, I met a man who told me how his son had just taught him a lesson about bullying. The little boy was having trouble on the bus because another boy was picking on him. The father advised him to punch the kid if it happened again. The next day, the boy reported that the bus ride was fine. His father had expected a blow-by-blow account and was stunned to hear his son's story.

"I didn't hit him," the boy told his dad. "I made him my friend."

Who would've guessed that a grown man would be learning such a valuable lesson from a five-year-old boy?

This approach has been the work of Israel (Izzy) Kalman, Nationally Certified School Psychologist, who developed Bullies to Buddies. It also exemplifies the work of Brooks Gibbs, father, and author of *Love Is Greater Than Hate*.

When I told Brooks the story of the little peacemaker on the bus, he wasn't surprised. "Smart kids learn really quickly that the key to stopping mean behavior is to stop being mean back," he said. "The solution is found in the Golden Rule: treat others the way you want to be treated. Don't treat them the way they treat you.

"Dr. Martin Luther King Jr. said it best when he preached that 'Hate cannot drive out hate, only love can do that,'" Brooks continued. "Abraham Lincoln asked, 'Do I not destroy my enemies when I make them my friends?' Wise people throughout the centuries and philosophers throughout the millennia have made logical proofs that the way you stop mean behavior is by refusing to be mean back. It's not children who have a hard time understanding this; it's the adults in their life who struggle to exemplify this fundamental ethic."

Redefining "Stepping Up" for Kids

Should we be telling kids to *stand or step up* to bullies? According to the kids who participated in the Youth Voice Project, this is what helps and what doesn't:

Most Helpful Peer Actions

- Spent time with me, sat with me, or hung out with me
- Talked to me at school to encourage me
- Helped me get away from situations where the behavior was going on
- Listened to me
- Gave me advice about what I should do
- Called me at home to encourage me
- Helped me tell an adult
- Distracted those who were treating me badly
- Told an adult
- Asked the person to stop being mean in a friendly way

Least Helpful Peer Actions

- Told the person to stop in a mean or angry way
- Ignored what was going on
- Made fun of me for asking for help or being treated badly
- Blamed me for what was happening

Tangled Ball® Leadership Skills

With all of this in mind, and with the intention of creating young leaders among our children, we can establish a clear foundation for what types of behavior will accomplish those goals. Here are our top picks for golden rules to make that happen.

#1: Being Respectful

Please. Thank you. You're welcome. Excuse me. Sorry. Sharing. Picking up toys and clothes. Not interrupting.

I did fairly well with most of that—except for the not interrupting part. When my kids would interrupt my conversation with another adult, I'd ask them to wait but I wouldn't follow through. Two seconds later, they would interrupt again so I would stop my conversation to talk with them.

This drove my dear brother-in-law, Cliff, crazy so he took matters into his own hands. When the kids would do it in front of him, he would firmly—very firmly—stop and tell them that they had to leave the room. They could not, under any circumstance, unless someone broke an arm or fell down a flight of steps, interrupt. They quickly reformed and I did, too.

I learned a lot from Cliff. He was not a formal educator but the one word I'd use to describe him is teacher. He taught our children how to fish, camp, ride a bike, drive "Little Blue" (the family's favorite tractor), split wood, work in an office, mow a lawn, and of course—not interrupt. That last one is something he especially liked. I promised him before he died that his nieces and nephews would carry on his legacy of respect, and they have; that's for sure.

#2: Building on Personal Strengths

Kids can be funny, smart, bold, kind, or quietly confident. Sometimes, they possess some other wonderful trait that we are not aware of, not because we underestimate them; it could just be because we haven't seen it in action yet.

When it comes to diffusing difficult situations, we must encourage our children to use their strengths and imagination. Not every tangled ball can be unraveled in a conventional way. In other words, if your child has a sense of humor, they should use it to diffuse tension in a good-natured way. When they do so, they should be recognized and complimented for diffusing a tricky situation—for themselves or another child—in any way they can pull it off. Nurture their kindness, boldness, sensitivity, and emotional intelligence—whatever they've shown that works to promote a good social climate in their classroom, playground, synagogue, church hall, or home.

Peers can show support by going to a teacher for help, making eye contact with the target, or slipping in a word of sympathy. If they have the confidence to say stop without being confrontational, that will certainly matter. If they make a joke or do something funny, it can change the mood and focus. If they do not join with the crowd to bully someone, this could be considered support, and also takes character, and they should be encouraged.

Every child has something positive to contribute.

Take the example of 14-year-old Robby Novak, aka Kid President. When he was nine, he started to share his wisdom in hysterical internet videos. He and his older brother-in-law Brad Montague are on a mission to inspire a joyful revolution and to spread the word to treat everyone like it's their birthday every day. Robby is inspirational in more ways than one. He suffers from *osteogenesis imperfecta*, also known as *brittle bone disease*, and has endured over 70 broken bones and multiple operations. But that doesn't stop him from dancing.

His light-hearted attitude and words of wisdom make him one of the most effective leaders at any age. His Soul Pancake YouTube videos are worth the watch and have been viewed by millions around the world.

#3: Nurturing Empathy

Like most any subject matter, teaching empathy can be creative. What makes it stand apart is how essential it is, as much as math and reading and writing. I only wish more schools would give it the attention it deserves and spend more time focusing on this emotional lifeline to goodness and harmony. Meanwhile, it's up to parents to fill the gaps with their own brand of educating their children about the necessity and merits of genuine empathy.

"It's kind of like weight training," says Dr. Richard J. Davidson of the University of Wisconsin. "We found that people can actually build up their compassion 'muscle' and respond to others' suffering with care and a desire to help."[10]

Here are several tips for introducing the concept of empathy and building on it.

- Using children's books, play the "What would *you* do?" game. Ask kids what they would do in certain situations if they were a character in the book. Do the same with television shows and movies.
- Get involved in outreach projects and let them participate. Empathy demonstrated through action feels powerful.
- Watch videos like *Kid President*.
- Encourage your kids to use their talents to turn bad circumstances around at school, on the bus, on the field, or at after-school activities.
- Let children take care of a family pet.
- Notice their kindnesses and talk about it. (See RandomActsofKindness.org)
- If you're tired or could use some help, ask

---

[10] Source: RandomActsofKindness.org—Collection of Ideas to Build Empathy in Our Little Ones.

your kids to do small things for you. Let them know how they helped.

- Teach kids how to write a note to someone who could benefit from the attention, such as a grandparent. (Note: I am a grandparent.)
- Celebrate "Be Nice to the New Kid Week." It's what I always called the first week of school. It's an annual opportunity for kids to be empathetic.
- Do activities like the ageless Crumpled Paper Exercise, created by a teacher who wanted to give a classroom lesson on the lasting negative impact of mean behavior.

CRUMPLED PAPER EXERCISE

Step 1: Hand out a clean sheet of paper and ask kids to admire it. They can draw a simple heart on it if they wish.

Step 2: Ask them to crumple it. They can even stomp on it but ask them not to rip it.

Step 3: Ask them to smooth it out, trying to make it as perfect as it was when they started.

The Lesson: It's impossible. That's what happens to someone's heart when we're mean.

#4: Communicating and Expressing Themselves

When my oldest daughter, Alice-Kate, graduated high school, I felt like I swallowed bricks. I couldn't bear how much I was going to miss her. When it came time for toasts at the luncheon, I stood up to say a few words. What I thought were very poignant sentiments about her wonderful four years and my hopes for her next steps came out of my mouth sounding more like a small animal being tortured. Family and friends assured me afterward that no actual words were uttered and if I thought I may not have expressed myself quite the way I wanted, I was right. No one had any idea what I was trying to say.

Children face the same thing sometimes when they are overcome with emotion. It takes a lot of listening and translating. They could be saying one thing but the real issue may be too intense to decipher because of frustration, anger, or jealousy. They need help getting to the bottom of it.

"Are you really mad because _____?"
"Were you a little scared because _____?"
"Could you be frustrated because _____?"

We need to help kids find words for what they are feeling and then they can deal with it. This is called Social and Emotional Learning (SEL), a process through which children and adults acquire and effectively apply the knowledge, attitudes, and skills necessary to understand and manage emotions, set and achieve positive goals, feel and show empathy for others, establish and maintain positive relationships, and make responsible decisions.

SEL programming is based on the understanding that the best learning emerges in the context of supportive relationships that make it challenging, engaging, and meaningful.[11]

Developing SEL skills at home doesn't have to be boring. *Kid President's Guide to Being Awesome* has 100 ways to avoid that. It offers ideas ranging from How to Hold a Socktober in Your Town to Solve a Conflict Using Ice Cream.

A Positive Opportunity

Bullying prevention can be one huge learning opportunity, particularly when kids are testing the social waters.

---

[11] CASEL (Collaborative for Academic, Social, and Emotional Learning, accessed at casel.org).

According to "Preventing Bullying in Childcare Settings," posted online by EyesonBullying.org, "To prevent bullying from escalating, caregivers can prepare themselves with effective strategies to deal with bullying incidents–before, during, and after they occur. They can also look ahead and take steps to create an environment that supports respect, where bullying is neither accepted nor tolerated. Finally, caregivers can help children learn the social skills they need to deal effectively with bullying, when it occurs.

"To gain and maintain friends and avoid becoming involved in bullying, young children need to learn a variety of social skills. They must learn how to analyze and resolve social problems, understand and respond caringly to what others think and feel, and stand up for themselves in a fair and respectful way, without attacking others."[12]

In general, most aggressive behaviors we see from young kids would not technically be considered real bullying but they do exhibit the seeds of behavior that may evolve and cross the line.

Dr. Ron Slaby offers the example of the child who aggressively grabs a ball away from another child. The goal is to get the ball but the side result is that the other child cries and nearby children watch. This aggressive behavior is not yet bullying because it is not yet done intentionally, repeatedly, and for the purpose of asserting power over another. But if allowed to continue, a new goal may become to make the other child repeatedly cry because it makes the aggressor feel powerful and it impresses the other kids, who start to do the same thing. It's repeated and becomes a bullying game in itself. What started out as a child's simple failure to get a ball in a cooperative, nonaggressive way—if not corrected—can become a repeated power play that rapidly spreads throughout the group.

---

[12] Slaby, R.G., & Storey, K.S. (2008), *The Eyes on Bullying Program* (online).

What About Teasing?

What might begin at home among siblings can become toxic in a public environment. Teasing in the household might be part of a family's culture but when it spills over to the classroom some kids don't react well. A little sensitivity training here can go a long way.

While it's important to learn not to take everything too personally, for many children, it's a process. Kids adapt to teasing pretty quickly, either teasing others or putting their own selves down before anyone else has the chance. Personally, I'm not a huge fan of humor with an edge but some good-natured teasing has a purpose.

Consider the average klutzy kid trying to ice skate who keeps falling. If they are not put down and the skill of learning is treated in a good-natured way, most children will learn how to laugh at their slip-ups and will be more determined to get up and try again. This may also help them become more sensitive to others.

It's always helpful to have a thick skin but we must also understand that some children are just more emotional than others. Working with them on their confidence goes a much longer way than expecting them not to take something personally when they feel like they are on shaky ground. Perhaps all they need in those cases is a firm foothold.

To learn more about this, try reading *The Optimistic Child* and *Learned Optimism,* both by Dr. Martin E. P. Seligman, the director of the Positive Psychology Center at the University of Pennsylvania. His writing was invaluable to me when my children were young. He provides ways to encourage confidence and optimism from the inside out.

How Do Children See Themselves?

The *Ordinary People Change the World* series can inspire children from kindergarten through 4th grade by viewing great leaders in our history as they lived as children. After all, Abraham Lincoln, Albert Einstein, and Rosa Parks were children before they became great figures in the world.

After a group of 3rd graders read the books, they were asked to identify leadership traits they have in common with the famous people they read about. Then they wrote their own autobiographies, imagining themselves as adults and reflecting on their childhoods. The beauty of this exercise, which parents can also do at home with their kids, is that they placed themselves in their own story as a leader. Here are a few examples of what these children wrote:

"I was born in 2007 and I was a leader. When anyone needed help I would help them. If they were sick, I would pay to take who is sick to the doctors. When I was four, I wanted to help everyone. When my mom hurt her back me and my dad helped her. I am the best kid who is a leader." —*Isaiah (St. Adalbert School)*

"I always wanted to be a baker because my mom was a baker, too. I learned to bake from watching my mom cook and bake. I would always make a baked treat and give some to my family and friends. Me and my mom enjoyed watching baking shows, baking magazines, and cook books. When I was nine I started to make breakfast for my family like pancakes and scones. Soon I wanted to start making cake mix but only four people bought it. Then I started to sell cakes for graduation and made $50 from it."
—*Sophia (P.S. 29 Bardwell School)*

"I do rights, talk, read, write, teach people how to ride or drive things like scooters, bikes, skating boards, cars, motorcycle, and horses."
—*Aaron (St. Adalbert School)*

"I would put on tons and tons of little shows whenever I could. My grandma came to my house a lot for dinner so I would really sing from the heart."   —*Scarlet (P.S. 29 Bardwell School)*

Leadership According to 3rd Graders

When I asked a group of children at St. Adalbert's Elementary School about what they thought about the idea of leadership, the words and phrases they used to describe this quality were telling.

Bravery
Smart
Helpful
Friendly
Courage
Generous
Enthusiasm
Working Hard
Let people sit with you
Teach people how to be kind
Do something good so others will do it, too

Who could argue with any of these kids? They know what to do, and most of them have it in their hearts to do the right thing. Maybe we should wrap those capes around their shoulders and follow the leaders.

Leadership is the anti-bully.

Tangled Ball® Worksheet

On those days that you've had to correct your child 45 times or you expect them to brush their teeth without reminding them and they don't do it, or they embarrass you in front of the one person who has a "perfect" child, you may not think that you are raising a leader. But you are. Good job. Take a moment to think about your children and what *raising leaders* means.

Q: Is there such a thing as a born leader? Is leadership teachable? If so, why? If not, why?

_____

_____

_____

Q: Leadership is the anti-bully. Agree? Disagree?

_____

_____

_____

Q: *Ordinary People Change the World*. What do you think of this idea?

_____

_____

Q: Is empathy teachable? If so, do you have tips for other parents?

_____

_____

Q: Does technology help or hinder nurturing positive leadership skills in our children?

_____

_____

STRING FOUR

STRING FOUR

Tools for an Emotional Roller Coaster

Sorting out the tangled strings of our own emotions can be daunting, let alone those of our growing and unpredictable children. Luckily, many creative initiatives and teaching tools exist for parents and educators that help sort out the subtle and not so subtle emotions our kids experience every day and sometimes on an hourly basis.

The Yale Center for Emotional Intelligence conducts research and develops innovative approaches to teach people of all ages the emotional skills they need to live healthy, happy, and productive lives.

Emotions matter.

This tagline—which sums up the Center's mission—exemplifies what researchers have found over the past two decades: that emotions affect the ability of children and adults to learn, make sound decisions, make and keep friends, and maintain effective habits early in life, leading to success at work and in intimate relationships.

The Mood Meter

We can see the range of how children use emotions to achieve their goals in the five skills of emotional intelligence:

1. Recognizing emotion in self and others
2. Understanding causes and consequences of emotions
3. Labeling emotions accurately
4. Expressing emotions appropriately
5. Regulating emotions effectively

These skills comprise the Center's RULER approach to social and emotional learning, one that has been embedded into some public and private pre-K, elementary, middle, and high schools.

Among the RULER tools is a downloadable app called the *Mood Meter*. It fosters emotional intelligence by inviting people to observe their emotion patterns, increase their emotional vocabulary, and learn effective strategies to manage emotions. It also provides a report so that people can observe their emotional patterns over time.

According to Robin Stern, PhD, associate director of the Yale Center for Emotional Intelligence and a principal investigator for the RULER for Parents project, "The Mood Meter has been very useful and fun... the app makes 'checking in' immediate and easy, and the reminders are helpful in establishing the practice of 'checking in' with yourself. Using the app reinforces all the skills of emotional intelligence and has sparked many conversations with my kids about the value of nuanced emotion vocabulary, about what it means to have a choice to use a regulation strategy or not, and about the benefit of knowing your personal emotion patterns and triggers, and about having a positive mindset about the value of emotions."

TOOLBOX

TOOLBOX™, created and written by Mark A. Collin and distributed by Dovetail Learning[13], is based on their research and discovery that young learners from kindergarten through

---

[13] DovetailLearning.org.

6th grade possess the innate capacity and ability to tap into and strengthen their own social-emotional well-being by helping them to identify 12 inner "tools" or strategies. By using the metaphor of a 'toolbox' and 'tools'—such as listening, empathy, courage, apology, and forgiveness—children begin to take ownership of their thoughts and behaviors.

Active Listening

It seems that the entire world is suffering from attention issues. With so many distractions, it may be getting harder and harder to be a good listener or to know one. It's a skill that can be learned, though, and for those who master it, it can do wonders.

You can explain to your children that when someone they know is being bullied, they probably want someone to talk to as a friend. Research shows that pre-teens and teens want to talk to their peers first, which is another good reason to start raising leaders from a young age. They will soon be the Go-To-Teens for other teens.

Helping our children learn how to listen can start with eye contact and using people's names, as well as role-play, using books as tools, practice, repetition, focusing, and praise. We might even share with our kids the words of Ernest Hemingway, who said, "When people talk, listen completely; most people never listen."

The Importance of Eye Contact

Encouraging children to make eye contact will serve them well for the rest of their lives. It comes easily to some and not so easily for others, but it's one of the best skills to learn for the following four reasons:

1. It sends a signal that you are focusing on what the other person is saying.

2. It can be an effective assertiveness tool. In the event they need to stick up for themselves, making eye contact and saying stop can be a potent combination.

3. It comes in handy as a sign of support. Some children can't step up and intervene in a mean situation. Instead, giving the target sympathetic eye contact can help blunt the pain and make the target feel less isolated.

4. It's an invaluable tool when your child is the one in the wrong. Making eye contact and apologizing can also be a potent combination.

The reverse is also true and should be discussed. As kids get older, purposely not making eye contact can become a weapon, and when used in a mean-spirited way, it is one of the worst forms of bullying. It's an effective weapon because while it diminishes the other person, it's hard for that target to call it out.

Once children learn this, it's hard to unlearn. Have you ever had an employer or co-worker treat you okay in front of others but never looked at you? This passive-aggressive trick can feel like torture. That mean manager who wields their power over others was once a child.

Making eye contact means connecting, which is the main pathway to listening. It's also fundamental to showing respect and being able to communicate effectively. If a child has trouble making eye contact, get down on their level and look them in the eye, while encouraging them to do the same with others.

The simple and powerful act of making eye contact shows how you value another person and helps immensely in creating positive interactions with others. It has a powerful ripple effect. That's leadership.

Using People's Names

Addressing people by name, coupled with eye contact, is also a powerful combination.

Many of my friends' kids are trained by their parents to call an adult by their name as they are being greeted or when saying goodbye. It's very endearing and sets up immediate communication. This skill of connecting yields three benefits:

1. Calling people by their names makes them feel seen.
2. Being seen makes people feel valued.
3. Feeling valued makes people feel important.

Needed: Extra Dose of Love and Support

These skills—active listening and making eye contact—can be especially hard for parents of children with any type of physical, mental, emotional, or learning challenge. What's entailed in these situations is worthy of its own book. There are ways to support parents who have their hands full making sure their children are included. All parents need other Go-To Parents, but it's especially true for those who have extra layers of worry. For these parents, we might do well by sharing our capes every now and then.

Organizations like Understood, for parents of the one in five children with learning and attention issues, and the PACER Center, champions of children with disabilities, are particularly good resources for parents with children of special needs, as well as friends and family who want to support them.

Developed by 15 nonprofits, Understood.org is a free resource for parents of kids with learning and attention issues empowering these parents to help their kids reach their full potential. Challenges like ADHD and dyslexia may not only affect a child's academics, but can also impact confidence and social skills. Understood has thousands of resources on everything from the evaluation process, treatment options, and teaching approaches to managing daily routines and relationships. Free daily online events connect parents with experts in the field, and the online community is a great source of ideas and support from other parents. Its mission of creating community is captured in its name: Understood.

Amanda Morin, a writer and staff expert at Understood, expresses their mission: "One in five kids in the U.S.— including mine—have a brain-based learning or attention issue. That includes issues like dyslexia and ADHD that can affect reading, writing, math, attention, and organization. I know as a parent and as an expert that these kids can thrive in school and in life with the right support. Understood's goal is to help parents like me help their children unlock their strengths and reach their full potential. At Understood.org direct access to chats with experts, an online community of other parents, and thousands of personalized resources and practical tips on topics from bullying to study skills help parents know we're not alone."

The nonprofit PACER Center, a parent training and information center, was established to help parents of children of all disabilities from birth to young adulthood, including physical, mental, emotional, learning, and health challenges. They discovered that, sadly, another challenge for students was mistreatment by peers. They decided that they needed to take action so that schools were safe for all children. PACER's National Bullying Prevention Center was created and is now a leader in the field.

"The students themselves are catalysts for change," says Julie Hertzog, director of PACER's National Center for Bullying Prevention. "As they are the ones experiencing the bullying, they know the social hierarchies and dynamics, and involving them in the solution is critical. But they can't do this alone. Bullying prevention is everyone's responsibility, and students need to know that they are supported by adults and teachers. Social change happens when everyone is involved, that adults are also taking action and that there is an infrastructure in place through legislation, policy, and education. When we stand together, no one stands alone."

The Small Stuff

Even something as ridiculous as wearing the wrong clothes can attract mean comments. For instance, my son's friend always wore black. His mother, Ariel, admitted to not caring much about clothes so she hadn't even noticed until he was getting snide remarks. He wasn't trying to be

Goth, especially since he was only eight. He just needed new clothes to avoid getting hassled at school.

When the same boy turned 13, someone gave him a hard time for his sneakers. Having learned from previous experience, Ariel decided to nip this in the bud and buy shoes that would be her son's ticket back to inclusion. Halfway to the mall, he made her turn around because he refused to get that shallow.

Ariel learned a lesson that day from her son. He was getting older and it wasn't her problem to fix this for him, unless he needed a ride to the store.

More Tangled Ball® Tips

Role Play: Show your kids what it's like when you're not listening to them. Then demonstrate what it's like when they have your attention. They'll get the point. Once again, this is a powerful tool.

Good body language: Attentive looks much different than tuning out. This takes practice.

Read: How we read with our kids makes a difference. Stopping to ask questions or to have a dialogue about the story helps them develop thinking and listening skills.

Breathe and refocus: Also known as *mindfulness,* this technique is especially helpful when children are tired or not paying attention. A new research-based mobile-friendly app, called Mind-Yeti, was developed for families and classrooms by Committee for Children, a global non-profit dedicated to promoting social-emotional skills.

"Students are telling us they feel calmer immediately after using Mind-Yeti," says Mia Doces, Director of New Mission Ventures for Committee for Children. "That's really good news because a calm, focused mind can make a big difference in school performance, both socially and academically."

For example, asking kids to repeat instructions, such as "Please pick up your shoes in the living room, put them in the closet, get your math book, and bring down your pencils." When these phrases are repeated back to you, you know children are listening.

> *Praise:* When children listen, offer acknowledgment through praise, but make sure it's specific. For example, "You brought down your book *and* pencils. Good listening."

> *Bonus Tip:* Consider writing a letter to your child on his or her birthday that helps them recognize what special leadership traits they have. This makes a special day become an even better "I See You" day.

> *Dear [child's name]:*
> *Happy Birthday! On this important day, I want to tell you that you are a wonderful person. You are kind, you try hard and you are funny. As you grow up, I want you to use all of your great strengths to make the world a better place.*
>   *Love, Your Proud Parent*

Understanding What Works

Youth Voice Project: Student Insight into Bullying and Peer Mistreatment is the result of a reach-out campaign to more than 13,000 elementary school, middle school, and high school children which sought to find the answer to a burning question: What really works?

Stan Davis, a social worker, counselor, and co-author of *Schools Where Everyone Belongs: Practical Strategies for Reducing Bullying* and *Empowering Bystanders in Bullying Prevention,* and Charisse Nixon, PhD, researcher and author, describe a trend in telling elementary-aged students to stand up to bullies when they witness mistreatment.

"The most helpful peer actions," they say, "are those directed toward establishing a connection with mistreated students and helping them get away from the mistreatment. In fact, peer actions that provided connection and emotional support or distraction were rated by mistreated youth as more helpful than peer actions involving direct efforts to stop the mistreatment. Thus, approaches that encourage mentoring, inclusion, and emotional support are likely more promising than approaches that focus on teaching peers to 'say no to bullying' or 'stand up to bullies.' Mistreated youth in elementary school reported that the most helpful peer actions focused on providing support, helping to access adult support, and distraction. For both males and females, supportive actions such as 'talked to me at school to encourage me' and 'spent time with me' were overwhelmingly helpful."

These results are encouraging and give us a concrete direction on how we approach this issue with our children.

Tangled Ball® Worksheet

Communication plays a central role in effective parenting. It often begins with asking the right questions. The answers may be elusive, however, and remain fluid as our children grow. In fact, have you ever wished you could just open up their little heads and look inside? Some days they need a little rewiring to cope with growing up. But the more they come to understand themselves, the easier it is for us to help them with skill building.

Q: How do you help your kids learn how to identify their feelings?

_____

_____

Q: Can we help them sort out emotions such as frustration, sadness, and anger?

_____

_____

Q: What gets in the way of the art of listening?

_____

_____

Q: Eye contact and using people's names contribute to empowerment and connection. What other everyday skills can do the same?

_____

_____

Q: According to the Youth Voice Project, the most effective peer help is to create a connection with mistreated students. How can parents prepare kids to help others?

_____

_____

STRING THREE

STRING THREE

Why Kids Don't Tell
and How to Change That

Following the tragic suicide in 2003 of his 13-year-old son, Ryan, John Halligan made it his life's work to advocate for legislation to prevent bullying, cyber-bullying and suicide and to tell Ryan's story to as many middle school and high school students as possible. His hope is that by sharing his family's personal story and his son's silent struggles, pre-teens and teens will be inspired to be kinder on and offline, and tell a trusted adult when there's a problem.

"Bullied children often feel embarrassed for being bullied and are reluctant to seek help," says John. "Many times they feel adults may make matters worse because they don't always know how to approach the school administrators correctly.

"But what may feel manageable at the moment may build to a breaking point. It is critical we train school counselors, teachers and parents to handle bullying the right way so that we establish the trust and confidence of a bullied child."

It is more than likely that John has saved the lives of countless children through his tireless advocacy. We can learn valuable lessons from his work and apply that knowledge to situations that arise with younger children.

The Real Experts

This book leans on education, psychology, and technology experts, as well as other parents and mentors. But make no mistake. Kids are the real experts in their own world when it comes to social dynamics in the classroom, cafeteria, school bathroom, bus, or playground. It's humbling to know that these small adults-in-the-making are far more knowledgeable about what goes on in that world than we are.

We must be willing to learn from them first.

Several years ago, a school counselor and I gave an anonymous bullying survey to students in grades four through eight at a well-run, close-knit, neighborhood elementary school. We were beginning a new bullying prevention/leadership initiative and wanted to get an idea if bullying was an issue. I'm still grateful to the principal for giving us the go-ahead. As an administrator, it takes courage to seek the truth. Like me, she also did not think there was any problem.

Shockingly, about one-third of the students, which just about mirrors national statistics, felt that bullying impacted them to some degree. Children as young as nine were writing notes at the top of the survey saying things like "Please Help."

It was painful to see. It begs the question, *how* do we help? In the short-term, kids suffering in silence just need the problem to stop. In the long-term, they need coping skills to help minimize these situations. In other words, they need support, and it all begins with communication.

Tell a trusted adult.

This is the most common piece of expert advice, including among those dealing with young children.

Most Frequent Reasons Why Kids Don't Tell

- *Shame:* According to youth and parenting expert Barbara R. Greenberg, PhD, co-author of *Teenage As a Second Language: A Parent's Guide to Becoming*

Bilingual, feeling shame—for being called "stupid," "fat," "ugly," "retarded," "gay," a "loser"—is one of the most difficult emotions to handle and can have long-term consequences.

- *Fear of things getting worse:* A child instinctively knows the power of the bully and often feels that "no one understands, so the bully will just win, no matter what." The target also knows that the bully is good at what he or she does.

- *Retaliation from the bully:* When a target tells another child or adult, it triggers responses like "You told? You jerk. Now you're really going to get it."

- *Fear an adult will overreact:* Children are often worried that one of their parents will call the parent of the bully and "give them a piece of my mind!"

- *Fear an adult will under-react:* Even worse, a child may think their pleas will be ignored.

- *Fear that they won't be taken seriously or believed:* We often hear kids report that "They think I make up things to be dramatic."

- *Fear they may be seen as a snitch:* Targets of bullying are frequently told not to tattle because if they do, everyone will hate them. This adds unbearable pressure for the target.

- *Fear that a cell phone and/or computer will be taken away:* "If I show anyone what these texts say," a child told me once, "I'll be blamed or they'll get scared and take my cell away or make me take down my page." Many kids are paranoid about this lifeline, that if they do not have it they will be out of the loop, which, for some children, may be even worse than the bullying.

- *Assumes an adult already knows:* Here we go with the superhero effect. Some kids think parents see, hear and know everything, and must be choosing to do nothing about the bullying. That compounds the issue on many fronts.

- *No one will actually do anything about it:* When a child says, "I told the teacher a bunch of times and she did nothing," then you have a bullying problem with a child and a serious trust issue with an adult. Both need fixing, and parent intervention is usually inevitable in this case.

- *They don't understand subtle acts of mistreatment:* According to Committee for Children, developer of Second Step, an SEL and bullying prevention program, students may not report more subtle, indirect, and relational types of bullying, such as deliberately excluding peers or spreading rumors, because they don't realize that these are unfair, unequal ways to treat others.

Red Flag

If your child is being harassed online, it's vital that you take action right away. Go to *StopBullying.gov* for immediate guidance. The first step is to make sure the child does not respond online. Teaching kids to immediately take their hands off any type of keyboard is a simple technique to ensure that matters don't get worse. The next step is to tell someone, and if the child tells you, compliment them for doing so, stay calm, and follow the cyber-bullying prevention and reporting advice that StopBullying.gov offers.

Keeping Communication Lines Open

Here is your challenge when it comes to peer-to-peer mistreatment, no matter what role your child occupies: React so they will come back. It's like playing the outfield in baseball. You never know when the ball is coming your way but you must always be prepared. This section presents multiple issues many of us will face. This might be a good moment to take your cape to the dry cleaners.

Shame versus Building a Feeling of Self-Respect: Low levels of dysfunction in a family contribute to feelings of self-respect and confidence while higher levels may cause low self-esteem. Here is a list of common actions by parents, siblings, or others that contribute to feelings of shame.[14] Just like many other childhood issues, shame is its own tangled ball.

Sarcasm	Belittling
Predicting failure	Ignoring
Raging	Swearing
Disparaging	Interrupting
Treating other kids better	Demeaning
Over-focusing on mistakes	Name-calling
Unrealistic expectations	Breaking promises
Discounting successes	Threatening
Comparing with ideal children	Never praising
Inappropriate touching	No touching

Bottom Line: Being aware and avoiding the actions on this list is a step toward creating a nurturing home where children understand the difference between the warmth of feeling valued and the cold and confusing feelings of shame.

Fear of Things Getting Worse versus Confidence That Things Will Get Better: A child instinctively knows the power of a bully. Bottom Line: Tread carefully. Listen. Strategize and follow through.

Retaliation from the Bully versus Feeling Safe: Kids who have mastered the art of being mean don't change overnight. You must understand that the target's fear of the bully holding on to their power is legitimate. Be realistic and help your child with ways to avoid repercussions.

---

[14] Courtesy of Peter K. Gerlach, MSW.

Resist the urge to give them simple advice on solutions they feel they can't pull off, such as "Just give 'em a good punch" or "Tell them they're a loser."

Some kids are picked on because they don't have an aggressive personality. Teaching a child to be properly assertive, being able to communicate what they need or want clearly, is a great skill. Telling or allowing them to be aggressive often lands them in the principal's office.

Avoid the word "just." That can be a red flag to your child that you don't understand what it's really like for them in the school setting.

Bottom Line: Sometimes it's better to help them avoid confrontation with the person being mean until a plan is in place.

Adult Overreaction versus Acting Like a Go-To Trusted Adult: First of all, recognize that your child is afraid, and that fear is a lousy thing to live with, especially when you're a kid. Try not to overreact. Take a few deep breaths and concentrate on listening to *everything* your child has to say. Even if you want to track down the child who is doing the bullying—don't. Your child is sharing what happened, but still needs to feel a semblance of control over the situation.

Overreacting can make matters worse. Kids are also easily embarrassed and seeing an adult come unglued isn't pretty. Plus, you may end up scaring the child and they'll be afraid to come to you again with a problem.

All of this takes practice, especially the breathing part. The only time most mothers are trained to breathe is preparing for childbirth. Who knew it was just a training session for getting through more challenging moments as they grow up?

Bottom Line: Most kids want your sympathy. They want to know someone cares.

Fear They Won't Be Taken Seriously versus Feeling Credible: When a child shares a story of bullying, they don't want to be told to ignore it, that it will go away by itself, because it probably won't and they know it! By telling them that, you invalidate their feelings and give them the impression that you do not believe them or take them seriously. In some cases, children know that the mean kid is so good at being mean that they have adults fooled.

Bottom Line: Believe your child until proven otherwise.

Fear of Being Seen As a Snitch versus Being Encouraged to Say What's Needed: Using the words *snitch, tattler,* or the phrase *Mind your own business* will backfire. These labels threaten the ability of children to be trusted by others. When kids don't tell an adult what's going on, it could very well be because they fear losing their friends and/or being assigned one of those labels.

Bottom Line: As mentioned earlier, telling a child not to tattle is common but potentially dangerous advice. Discourage kids from trying to get someone in trouble, but at the same time, teach them how to share information responsibly—and avoid labels.

Taking Cell Phones and Computers Away versus Feeling that Parents Won't Use Technology As a Disciplinary Tool: Be clear about cell and computer use before your children have access to both. That's where a contract helps. Websites such as CommonSenseMedia.org are great resources to prepare for that. Having rules and sticking to them reduces angst for both of you.

Bottom Line: Break the rules? Deal with the consequences. But kids shouldn't feel afraid to tell you if they've been on the receiving end of hurtful comments through texts or social media. And young kids should also be monitored to make sure they're not instigating negative drama or adding to the problem.

Assumes an Adult Already Knows versus Telling a Go-To Adult: For a child, it is highly frustrating to think that an adult with authority notices but doesn't do anything about behavior that is hurtful. It can feel hopeless. Kids trust that most adults are smart and see more than they do. Sometimes the only way we find out things about their world is to ask; the way we ask is critical.

Dr. Greenberg suggests that if you suspect there is bullying going on, asking kids a direct question, such as "Are you being bullied?" doesn't work. They can shut down. Asking an indirect question often works better, such as "Was recess fun today?" or "Are the kids in your class nice to each other?"

Bottom Line: They may not open up right away but wait patiently. They may want to talk to you when the focus isn't solely on them, such as when you're making dinner or working on the computer or even driving. Being in the car together is sometimes the most opportune time because you are both a captive audience for each other and your eyes are on the road and not uncomfortably on your kids as they reveal delicate information.

Not Understanding versus Becoming Aware of Boundaries: Some children simply don't understand when they're being mistreated.

Bottom Line: It's up to us to help them create boundaries and describe normal peer-to-peer behavior as opposed to letting kids take advantage of their lack of awareness.

Listening Tips for Superheroes

Let's begin with the assumption that your child may think you know more than you do. So why not begin by asking questions, listening, and showing your love and support? According to expert Elizabeth Lasky, PhD, LCSW, a specialist in teen bullying and cyber-bullying prevention, "What kids most want when they are being bullied is someone to talk to—a peer first and then an adult. And not necessarily to intervene, but just to listen and be supportive. Talk to your children and really listen to them. It is more important than you'll ever know."

I suggest beginning any conversation with turning off your cell phone and ignoring everything else around you.

Then don't speak. Let your child tell you what they're ready to report. Try not to interrupt. This is a time to find out the facts.

Most situations are not black and white. When they're through telling their story, ask questions without criticizing or judging. You may not approve of how they reacted, but save that for later. Stick to the facts and focus on their feelings.

Summarize the conversation when they've finished so they feel heard. For example:

Child: "It happens every time. They act like they're my friends, but when I go to sit at the table in the cafeteria, they act like there's no room, but then when someone else comes along, they let them sit there. I feel like they're laughing at me when I walk away. Everyone thinks they're so nice, but they're not nice at all."

You: "That's hurtful when people who you thought were friends aren't acting like it. Real friends don't leave you out on purpose."

Kids may stop assuming that you know things you don't when you say something like, "I'm happy when you tell me what's going on. That helps me understand" or "Does your teacher know?"

Creating a strategy is two-fold: Of course, try to get the bullying to stop. And equally, or perhaps more important, help blunt the pain that bullying causes by showing support.

Tangled Ball® Worksheet

No child should feel alone or suffer in silence. It breaks our hearts to even think that this is something our children might experience. Being aware of what they are feeling is the first step, and asking the right questions is part of that job.

Q: Considering the list of why kids don't tell an adult when they are being mistreated, did any surprise you? If so, why? If not, why? Would you like to add any others?

_____

_____

_____

Q: Based on your own experience, are there any other barriers to why kids don't tell?

_____

_____

_____

Q: As an adult, when we have an issue and need the help of other adults, how do we feel when that relative, friend, or colleague does not react in a helpful way? How do we support kids when the same thing happens to them?

_____

_____

_____

Q: Is having a basic strategy important in the event your child experiences some form of bullying?

_____

_____

_____

STRING TWO

STRING TWO

Schools Are Human, Too

Welcome back to school, your children's home away from home, in good times and bad.

The building is full of people just like you, anxious parents of young children, wanting everything to be perfect in this constructed village of families, professionals, and service workers. Each teacher and staff member has a life similar to yours—busy, full of daily tasks, with personal joys and setbacks along the way. In most cases, in order to accomplish everything necessary for success, they need support. I hope some of the advice you find here will help you create a roadmap for a healthy partnership with your children's school.

Belonging to Something Larger Than Ourselves

Building a strong and positive relationship with your school is essential. From your child's first day of school, the exchanges they have will form the foundation of how they will inevitably engage in their education, find value in who they are, and gain respect as part of the school community. This process begins with the connections each family makes with the school, and getting off on the right foot plays a pivotal role in developing trust and transparency, two essential components of any good relationship.

When asked, on a scale of 1 to 10, how important it is

to build a strong and positive home/school relationship, Darlene Faster, COO of the National School Climate Center (NSCC), says it's a 10!

"From a personal and professional perspective," she adds, "building a strong and positive home/school relationship is essential. Relationships are a foundational component to keeping students engaged, and helping them to feel valued and respected as part of the school community. This starts with the bonds that are built between the family and the school from day one, and it ensures the level of trust and open and honest communication that is necessary to meet the needs of each child."

Brené Brown, PhD, LMSW, takes it a step further. "We are profoundly social creatures," she says. "We may think we want money, power, fame, beauty, eternal youth or a new car, but at the root of most of these desires we find a need to belong, to be accepted, to connect with others, to be loved."[15]

This sense of belonging needs to be nurtured. Becoming a member of a community—like a school—is a privilege we must honor. It doesn't mean that you need to love—or even like—everyone in the community or everything about it, but its mission should align with yours. You are in this together, and there's safety in numbers. It really does take a village for children to become their best selves.

New Rules for School

1. *School administrators and teachers are people:* If you're nice, they tend to work *with* you. If you're not, they may lose patience. Never be mean to waiters, hairdressers—or teachers. In the end, they control what you eat, how you look—or whether your child likes school. Actually, most teachers are educators who will do

---

[15] Interview with Emma M. Seppälä, PhD, *Psychology Today* (2012; online).

what's best for your child no matter what, but the majority will respond better to a respectful approach.

(Also consider sending them a note when things go right. Everyone likes hearing something good occasionally.)

2. *Parenting is emotional:* Learn to breathe before talking. It will serve you well.

3. *If you want a problem solved, don't take your issues to the schoolyard:* Venting to a friend is different than sharing it with anyone who will listen. Kids tend to keep things to themselves if they think you are sharing it with others. When you usurp their story it makes them feel out of control, or it teaches them that gossiping about a problem is the way to go. Either result is unwelcome.

Case in point: A mother confided in me that she was trying to help her children navigate some pretty mean waters in school. Her oldest even had to switch classes, which was a painful decision. She noticed that if she picked her kids up early she became sucked into negative conversation that clouded her judgment. So she decided to volunteer in school at that time of day.

In the spirit of full disclosure, the situation didn't get better, but her ability to be objective and handle it with a clear head improved dramatically.

Donating Time and Talents

Getting involved in your child's school is time well spent. Three things in particular stand out to me about its value:

It makes your young kids feel important and proud.

It teaches them to get off the bench and into the game.

Putting your best foot forward will help the school do the same.

Finding time to volunteer may be difficult, but there are usually options, such as evening or weekend events. Showing up for anything you can helps you and the administration get to know each other, and you get a feel for how the school is run. Every school has its strengths and weaknesses. How can you contribute?

What to Do When Issues Arise

Hopefully, things will run smoothly for your children at school, but what happens when a situation arises? For example, when should you approach the principal or an appropriate staff member? The principal should be contacted when a problem becomes a pattern, and only after you've talked to the teacher and nothing has changed. You can also go directly to the top of the food chain if you think a situation is potentially damaging and needs an immediate course correction. This is critical because if these authority figures do not know what's happening, there is no chance for them to help.

Hopefully, the teacher is aware of the problem, but that is not always the case for a variety of reasons. It's best to stay realistic. Your child's issues may not be solved instantaneously but good communication will help.

Depending on how accessible the principal is, writing to him or her may be the best route. First, it gives you the chance to organize your thoughts, edit your choice of words, and be clear about what steps you would like the school to take. It also provides a record of what you've said.

Remember, one of the reasons kids don't tell adults is that they might have trouble communicating, especially if they're feeling emotional. In other words, it's mortifying for a child to start crying or just plain lose it in front of the principal. It's understandable, but embarrassing and non-productive. Chances are, you might be emotional, too, so make notes if you arrange a meeting in person and talk the situation through beforehand with a friend or someone you consider to be your own Go-To Adult.

I recommend heeding the words of Diane Hesterhagen, principal of St. Adalbert School in New York.

"Express anything—but it's all in the delivery."

Common Frustrations for Students and Parents

You can find many great professionals working in educational settings with the training and sensitivity to correct a situation.

In that case, you have an ally that will be able to handle whatever is happening without making things worse.

Then again, you may be unlucky and run into inertia and insensitivity on the part of a teacher and/or administrator. For example, it can be terribly frustrating for students and parents when a teacher or principal says they will address a problem but don't make much of an effort to follow through, or, if they do make attempts, they may be awkward and insensitively handled, leaving the student feeling even more vulnerable than before.

Conversely, some parents of the child causing the problem may brush it under the rug and won't take the bullying incident seriously. As a matter of fact, many parents find it hard to believe that their child has bullied someone. Sadly, some parents of kids who are exhibiting mean behavior may refuse to believe it and will defend their child. I call this type of behavior the "Not My Little Cupcake" syndrome.

This is frustrating, but not much can be done with this type of head-in-the-sand behavior. The only way to get through it is to go around the parent and get support from school staff.

Coping With an Imperfect Situation

Understanding a situation and acting accordingly should always include doing something that helps the child feel safe and loved. Once you ensure that is in place, you can put away your cape and begin to strategize about how to make it stop.

As a parent and child team, outline together what you want the school to know. It's best if you both communicate the facts without getting too worked up.

There is nothing worse than seeing a child feel demeaned, angry, sad, or defeated. It can be challenging to keep your own emotions in check. It can spark feelings of rage and can break your heart, but if you work together there is a tiny silver lining.

Whether you're going to talk to the school or send a letter, the process can benefit the child as well because it helps them build communication skills that will bode well for their future, while also allowing them to take back their power because being bullied inevitably compromises that.

A SAMPLE LETTER

Dear Principal, Teacher or Administrator,

I am writing this letter to express a concern I have regarding something my child, [NAME], is experiencing [in school, on the bus, in the cafeteria, etc.].

I would not reach out to you if I didn't strongly believe that this is a situation that needs your immediate attention.

[Briefly describe what has been happening— e.g., "my daughter/son is being harassed at recess by another child in his/her class"].

Please get back to me as soon as possible regarding a meeting time. If I don't hear from you within the next day, I will follow up with your office.

I know that we have the mutual interest of our children's mental, emotional, and physical health in mind, so thank you in advance for working with us to resolve this issue.

Sincerely,

[Both parents should sign the letter, if possible.]

Now What?

The principal or assistant principal gets right back to you, asking for the names of the children causing the problem and perhaps more detail. So what do you do?

Be honest. Tell the story in a factual way. Ask to have a meeting in person *without* the parents of the other student(s). Depending on how much you trust the principal or their skill with children, decide whether you want your child to be present.

Have a clear idea of what you want to happen. This makes the meeting more productive. Remember your end goal. Most parents just want a solution and having a meeting where you feel comfortable talking the issue through without accusations and anger will allow you to create an initial strategy and will help you gauge the school's level of genuine interest in finding a lasting solution.

If it is brought to your attention that your child is contributing to the negative situation, and they need to be corrected, keep an open mind. Avoid the urge to respond with "Not my child." First of all, he or she may actually be a normal kid who just acts out once in a while. Denying it is enabling, which is a recipe for disaster down the road. Accept that your child is a work-in-progress and do a course correction while they're still little and cute. Getting away with bad behavior becomes less and less cute as they grow.

If your child is truly innocent, the facts will prevail. Ultimately, you can tell if your child is telling the truth and if that's the case, go from there.

Either way, stay calm. Just because your sweet angel acts like a devil one day doesn't mean they'll be doomed to a life of crime when they get older—unless of course, you let them get away with too much bad behavior.

Kids like boundaries.

You may be the bad guy temporarily, but close your eyes and imagine that some day they'll win a huge award and start their acceptance speech with "Thank you, Mom."

After the meeting, write a thank-you note and recap what was said. Do it right away so you don't forget anything.

A SAMPLE RECAP NOTE

Dear Principal, Teacher or Administrator,

Thank you for your time this morning to discuss the situation. As you know, my concern is that it is beginning to affect [Jeannie's] desire to go to school, as well as her grades.

At the meeting, we discussed the possibility of the lunch monitors ensuring that Jeannie sit at a table with Imani and Alina. I would also like you to ask the recess monitors to keep an eye on Jeannie in the schoolyard.

Additionally, it would be very helpful if you would immediately move Jeannie's seat in class so that she is not sitting near the boys who have been bothering her.

I will work with Jeannie on not reacting when someone teases her. I had not realized that she was taking out her frustration on some of the other kids.

It is important to straighten this out right away, so I appreciate your cooperation.

Thank you again,

Mom in Jeans [Cape Optional]

Stay the Course

If things don't change within the next week, *follow up* and let the school know that you're holding up your end of the bargain. If things do not improve for your child, talk to someone in the school who will have your back. It could be a teacher or another administrator. If that doesn't work and you feel things will not get better even after addressing it through the proper channels, consider a change of classroom or school.

That's a huge decision and can be hard on you and your child, but sometimes it's the only choice you have. That's when you need the advice of experts, including counselors, other parents who have been down the same road, and professionals you trust.

Meanwhile, support your child in other ways. Work on getting them into activities where they meet other people. Perhaps trusted family members can help, too. Sometimes, you are their only friend, but if you hang in there, he or she will not feel alone.

No child should feel alone.

You can continue to help them identify their emotions so they can communicate. When they're acting out and frustrated at home, it may mean there's something going on at school. For example, anger at a sibling may be a result of feeling hurt by the actions of someone on the bus.

By the way, do not let siblings at home make it worse for the one who is struggling in school. A child needs to feel happy and safe at home.

Here's a good rule of thumb: Behavior that would be unacceptable between two unrelated children is unacceptable between two siblings. When one child intentionally and consistently hurts or frightens a smaller or less powerful sibling, that's bullying, and it needs to stop. Whether it happens with classmates or siblings, bullying can have long-term effects. It can damage self-esteem and set a pattern for abusive relationships.[16]

If you're like the thousands of other families who struggle with "sibling issues," best selling authors Adele Faber and Elaine Mazlish may be of help with their book, *Siblings Without Rivalry: How to Help Your Children Live Together So You Can Too.*

It can't hurt to remind your other children of the importance of not being cruel to others—under any circumstance. Even nice kids can be mean every now and then. When one sibling is getting too heavy with another, it may be a good time to put on your cape and issue a positive reminder, like "You know better than to treat people like that. I'm proud of you for being kind."

When things get stressed at school for your child, stay close to them and nurture their resilience. Continue to teach the skills of healthy assertiveness and stay the course.

Favorite Tips from Educators

I've met many caring principals, administrators, and teachers whose advice for other educators and parents is included here:

Training

If you're a teacher, counselor, or administrator, you may agree with most experts that training is key and that any program should be evidence-based and sustainable, and should include school staff and parents. It should also be fairly easy to implement and cost-effective.

Despite the fact that bullying is a complex problem that is handled best by comprehensive, multi-level interventions, educators often express a need for clear, concise, guidance in order to help them make informed decisions about choosing from the many bullying prevention and intervention programs available.

Visit the Alberti Center for Bullying Abuse Prevention

---

[16] CommitteeforChildren.org.

website and look for *Resources for Educators* for its *Guide to School-Wide Bullying Prevention Programs.* [17]

Creating Connections in School

Use the child's name, make eye contact, and ask questions that don't embarrass them, such as "Are you having a good day, James?" You'll know from their body language and response if they need to talk further.

Edutopia.org, sponsored by the George Lucas Educational Foundation, has amazing ideas about this for educators and parents.

Offer Safety

If kids are experiencing a big problem place them in a safe situation, such as giving them an alternative to eating in the cafeteria or going out to recess.

Promote Kindness

Seat a struggling child next to someone who is kind. Be sensitive to the child you choose. Even kind children find it hard to be responsible for another child. And let all kids know that if another child asks to sit next to them, the answer must almost always be yes.

Give Assurance

Let children know you are available and that they can always come to you.

Encourage Self-Reliance

Give kids simple tips for standing up for themselves, such as body language (stand tall), making eye contact, and asking for help when needed.

Build Leadership

Educators and parents can train and cultivate people, particularly bystanders, to be positive, considerate, and courageous leaders, aka Upstanders! As adults, we can make a conscious effort to stop negative behaviors and trends.

---

[17] gse.buffalo.edu/alberticenter.

"Through our model," says Paul Proscia, a New York City school principal and father, "children will learn to follow our lead as long as we assure them that we genuinely care, we can be trusted, and we can add value to them. We all have a Nelson Mandela, Abraham Lincoln, and Mahatma Gandhi in us."

Creating Mentors

When older kids teach younger ones, magic happens. The older ones take ownership of the message, while the younger ones feel safe. Although the older students are asked to help with the lower grades, they probably benefit the most because they have the chance to practice leadership.

The Youth Voice Project reports that student leadership programs have proven key in creating a sense of ownership and responsibility that empowers youth to change their social climate to one in which respect, kindness, and personal standards and character are the norm rather than the exception.

There are many leadership campaigns out there, such as The Leader In Me, based on Stephen R. Covey's highly popular *The 7 Habits for Highly Successful People,* or a school can create its own. One powerful thing all schools can do is to put children in leadership positions, however small.

Here are examples of initiatives you may find compelling.

Hometown Heroes: St. Adalbert's places a focus on veterans in its award-winning outreach campaign, *Hometown Heroes, a Living History Project.* Students interview local veterans about their military service, write up their stories, collect photos and supporting data, and publish the biographies. When the book is completed, the veterans are honored with a special celebratory breakfast. Every step in the process is a lesson in writing, history, listening, caring and leadership—and what a wonderful feeling for veterans.

LOCK (Leadership of Character for Kids): This is a leadership campaign developed by P.S. 29 Bardwell in New York to encourage students from kindergarten through 5th grade to practice good character. They are given multiple opportunities throughout the year to help organize and get involved in initiatives that positively impact the community.

"I personally have witnessed the difference in our students who are involved, who have succeeded in the challenges of their lives with assistance from their parents and teachers," says Elizabeth Ladiana, LOCK Coordinator at P.S. 29. "They are confident in themselves because they know they are not alone."

One Can Count: Co-developed with author Kathryn Otoshi, One Can Count is a mentoring tool based on Ms. Otoshi's ageless and powerful book, *One*. Older students are paired with younger students to read *One* as well as the other books in the series, *Zero* and *Two*. They discuss them and do simple creative activities together, such as word games and arts and crafts, which focus on the concept of character. The partnerships grow as they get to know and encourage each other. The bonds they create benefit both age groups, and it's fun. Go to TangledBall.com to download the curriculum materials for free.

Playground Mentors/AHM Youth and Family Services: Based in Hebron, Connecticut, AHM Youth and Family Services social workers and family therapists provide counseling services and positive youth development activities in public schools. Through their successful Playground Mentoring Program, middle school students mentor younger students during the younger students' recess times.

The expectations of the mentors are to be active role models, organize and play games, involve younger students in the games, and assist the students in solving common playground problems with guidance from adult mentors.

Maintaining Children's Confidence

It behooves us to remember that some kids don't tell their parents about being bullied because they feel shame or embarrassment. There's nothing worse than trusting someone and having that person share it with others without permission.

This isn't just something kids feel. If it's ever happened to you, you'll know how critical it is to resist the urge to talk about it with people who may not handle it with care. Because, as we know, betraying their confidence can almost be worse than the bullying itself.

During their research putting together *The Influence of Parent and Peer Attachments on Life Satisfaction in Middle Childhood and Early Adolescence* (2004), authors Amanda B. Nickerson, PhD, and Richard J. Nagle, PhD, found that parent trust was the best predictor of satisfaction with families.

One parent shared something with me that I have found all too common. She reached out by email to a couple of teachers regarding a sensitive issue with her child and other kids in the class. One of them took her request seriously about not sharing the contents of the email. The other teacher handled it poorly and asked the girl about it in front of the other students.

Needless to say, the mom was devastated when her daughter came home crying and recounted the story. Trust was eroded all around. Her daughter was not the only one who ended up in tears. All adults should respect confidence, but sadly, we have to be careful about how and what we communicate.

Honor your word.

If you say you're going to help, then follow through. They're counting on you. Being given false promises adds to the feeling of despondency. Feeling despondent leads to bad things. Being true to your word, builds trust. And trust leads to a feeling of security, which is a beautiful thing.

STRING TWO

Tangled Ball® Worksheet

Communication between parents and a school is like a dance. Sometimes we're in sync and other times we step on each other's toes. Our children win if both parties are committed to not sitting out the dance. Cue the music and take a moment to consider the following questions. You may have a few of your own, as well.

Q: Was bullying an issue when you were in elementary school? How was it handled? And did you have a Go-To Adult who you could turn to?

_____

_____

_____

Q: Are bullying prevention programs necessary for pre-K and kindergarten years?

_____

_____

Q: How should the issue be approached in elementary schools?

_____

_____

Q: What is normal sibling rivalry and when does it cross the line of mistreatment?

_____

_____

Q: What would you do if your "little cupcake" were caught being mean at school?

_____

_____

STRING ONE

STRING ONE

Gratitude and the Tangled Ball® Award

Sometimes we're related to our superheroes and sometimes they come into our lives in unexpected and amazing ways. While writing this book, I thought of all the people who seemed to suddenly appear at the right time and do the right thing. Although my childhood was generally a happy one, I wasn't fully aware of the importance of those big and small acts of kindness until I got older.

The Unexpected Go-To Adults

Luckily, people like April Houston Collins were on the receiving end of this kindness at a young age and did something about it. Years earlier, when April was only 13, she was named "Youth of the Year" by the Boys & Girls Clubs of North Alabama board of directors, when local businessman, Christopher H. Russell served as president.

Besides her triumphs as a scholar, citizen, and leader, April was also a caretaker in her family. Chris instinctively knew she could have a bright future if she had encouragement and positive role models in her life. He stepped up.

Fast forward. As April, the surprise guest speaker for the event, walked on to the stage, Chris sat stunned. Her surprised Go-To Adult, along with 800 others in a crowded ballroom for a major annual fundraiser, got to hear how one person can impact another and change the course of their life.

April removed a small, worn piece of paper from her pocket, and as part of her speech she read the note Chris had written to her, which she had saved all those years.

Dear April,

I wanted to write you a note to say thank you for speaking to the Athens City Council on behalf of the Boys & Girls Club.

For being so young, you exhibited tremendous leadership qualities. I think the reason you were so compelling to listen to is because you spoke from the heart. Most people older than you still have not learned that important lesson.

Try to hold onto the memory of that council meeting…value it as a stepping stone in your journey because you showed great character. With the maturity I saw you display at that meeting—and at your age—I think anything is possible.

Your friend,
Chris

Anything is possible. The first in her family to go to college, April is now an attorney with her own practice and a beautiful family. No surprise here, April is paying it forward.

A Belated Thank You

We don't always acknowledge the people who hung in there with us through thick and thin. For example, I often wish I had told my own mother more often how much her insight and love meant to me. Sometimes you just don't understand this until you're doing the same things for your own children.

My peers and I often say that we wish we had been more aware of what our parents did for us. In that spirit, on the following pages I share a letter from a daughter to her mother. It was never sent, but her feelings of gratitude remain important and powerful.

Dear Mom,

Thank you. It's taken a while but as I stand in Target with Billy and Kate's new school supply lists in hand, I suddenly understand the mixed-up feelings of sending little ones off to school. Part of me can't wait until they board that bus and I can have a couple of hours to myself, but the other part wants to keep everything exactly the same. Why can't we just go to the library and play with clay for the rest of our lives?

I want their little spirits to soar. They are full of enthusiasm so I cringe at the thought of anyone diminishing them. I know it happens, because it happened to me.

Those days when you handled me with care are the moments I now realize were filling up the little holes that other people poked in my heart. They weren't obvious from the outside. I was a smiley kid, so no one knew what was going on inside me. That's the problem. I didn't know why people were trying to make me feel bad. I still can't figure it out. At first I thought, "that's mean," but when more people started calling me fat and stupid, I started feeling ugly and dumb. I was afraid to open my mouth.

The funny thing is, I started to get a little chubby. When I got home from school, I couldn't wait to eat—and eat and eat and eat. I'll never forget the day I snuck away with a whole sleeve of Chips Ahoy chocolate chip cookies and ate them all!

When you would ask how my day went, I always said "fine." It was embarrassing and I was confused. Up until fifth grade, I actually liked school and had a lot of friends. My teachers were nice, but I started feeling self-conscious about raising my hand. I was scared about the parent-teacher meeting and couldn't think of anything else all day. I was afraid I'd get in trouble for not participating. Instead you told me you had a good conversation with Mrs. Thompson. Suddenly, I felt much lighter.

Our conversations in the car were the best. Even though

your eyes were on the road, I felt like you were looking into my heart. You picked up on little things, like when I wasn't invited to someone's house. You would make me laugh, and without sounding too mean, you would say things about the kids who ditched me. I'm not sure how you knew, but if you were guessing, you were really good at it.

Instead of calling me fat, you took me shopping for some clothes that would make me feel good, but even adults would make comments about my weight. There was the time our whole family was asked to a really nice party. I went there all happy until Mr. McGarren told me that I should "watch it, because you're getting a little chunky." It ruined my whole day. I wanted to hide until it was time to go home. It always surprised me. Why did they even care? You seemed to think I looked nice.

My happiest days were being a part of the children's theatre. You drove me there and back so many times during the week. That must have been hard. You had other kids and Gerry was a handful. (Sorry, Gerry, but you were.) Now, I'm not really sure how you did it. You were working part-time and doing all this other stuff for us but we all thought that it was normal. That's just what moms do. It really helped, though. It was such a great distraction and I met other kids. I also felt like they wanted me there. As an actress, I stunk, but they let me help with the set design and even lighting. I was only 10!

I got through the teen years, though not without a few bumps. But you tried to teach me not to take myself too seriously. Not easy, since I was a bit dramatic. Ironic.

I didn't tell you everything, but at times you seemed to have mental telepathy. I'm not sure how we got through the days when my emotions were all over the map and you were over it. But even when you were angry with me, you always got past it. And of course, I was always right, remember?

Looking back at old photos, I'm perplexed. I looked

fine. When I dug out my old report cards, it was right there in ink. I got good grades. Not Harvard material but not bad at all.

Just being there and listening helped plug up those nasty little holes I didn't deserve. As a matter of fact, it made me realize that no one deserves that. It gave me courage to be a better friend, except for the day when you caught me ditching Angela. You were so mad. You even made me call her to apologize.

I'm glad I had those experiences. If I didn't, I wouldn't know that taking a spin in the car to have a chat, or looking into my kids' souls when I notice that they don't seem like themselves, can be as much of a course corrector as giving a time out.

I know that some people may try to test my children's confidence but I can step in to help them see all they have to offer. I guess I have to be as accepting as you that they'll be clueless about the love and patience being poured into them. This can be a thankless and exhausting job, for sure.

I'm sorry I didn't have my light bulb moment sooner. Knowing that all those acts of kindness made the biggest difference would have given you a boost.

If I do my job right, one day I might also get a letter like this. Most likely, I'll have to be content with knowing that my kids feel good about themselves and can look at the bad days in the rearview mirror with a genuine smile.

Brace yourself. This will be a shock. I can finally say that I want to be just like my mom when I grow up.

Love,
Marie

P.S. We've just spent 20 minutes picking out a backpack. Was I this picky? On second thought, don't answer that.

One Final Note

Thank you for reading this book and talking about it with the other cool people in your life. I hope you have found more than enough trusted resources and warm connections to useful information.

Joy is everything. It doesn't depend on every day going right. It depends on appreciating the journey. As soon as your baby appeared in the world, chances are life became less predictable but much richer. Often, it became a tangled ball we can unravel only one string at a time.

That reminds me of two kids' jokes I read years ago:

"What's easy to get into and hard to get out of?"
Trouble.

"What did one hair say to the other hair?"
It takes two to tangle.

I hope that the Go-To Adults in your life will assist you with the knots as you help your children untangle a few strings of their own.

May you have fulfilling days, stress-free nights, and happy years ahead. If I could do a group text to all of you, it would simply say this:

> Enjoy the journey. You are not alone.
> In gratitude,
> Susie
>
> (No need to text back.
> They're coming home from school now.)

And as for the Tangled Ball® Award I referred to in the introduction, I think it's fair to say that everybody wins—if you choose to participate, which of course you do, because you are a superhero in mom jeans.

STRING ONE

Tangled Ball® Worksheet

Looking Back... and Moving Forward

Q: Have superheroes come into your life in unexpected and amazing ways?

_____

_____

_____

_____

_____

_____

Q: What would you like to say to them?

_____

_____

_____

_____

_____

Q: We are always looking for new perspectives in our anti-bullying/leadership campaign. Do you know of any resources you'd like to share? If so, please contact me and I will pass on the information through our website--www.tangledball.com.

_____

_____

_____

_____

_____

_____

_____

Acknowledgments

To the many professional individuals, organizations and educators who have taken on the issue of peer mistreatment: Thank you for lending your expertise, time, money, skills, and voice to support the wellbeing of our children. Your varied talents and perspectives help unravel problems that impact the heart. Your devotion and high-quality resources are enriching young lives.

To the professionals who took great care with the editing and design of the book: Thank you for lending your talents to helping young families navigate the journey of parenthood. Thanks, too, to my personal book support team for your continuous and invaluable insight, good humor and encouragement:

Barbara Shields
Karrie Ross
Nancy DeMuro
Cyndy Salgado
Danielle DiLillo
Anthony Zagame
Dominick's Bakery & Café Staff
Allen Mogol
Lisa Barone
Laurie Warren Guido
Elena Horohoe
Houston Rivero
Students and Staff at St. Adalbert School
Students and Staff at P.S. 29 Bardwell School
Family and Friends

...and to all the Superhero Moms (and Dads!) who shared their stories for this book.

About the Author

Susan S. Raisch is the founder of Tangled Ball®, a service that develops bullying prevention and leadership tools, including a website devoted to providing these resources for families and educators.

Before becoming a bullying prevention and leadership advocate, Susan was a public relations and public affairs consultant for more than 25 years, specializing in issues that affect the home, education, and health. She has worked on projects for a wide variety of television and publishing companies, including HBO, MTV, Sesame Workshop, Scholastic, and HISTORY, among many others. She also currently works with the Fire Department of the City of New York (FDNY) in the WTC Health Program, which treats and monitors the health of the FDNY certified 9/11 first responders.

She is married with four children and two grandchildren.

More About Tangled Ball®

To be continued…

For the full list of the high-quality resources found in this book, as well as others, please visit

TangledBall.com

To share *your* favorite bullying prevention and leadership ideas and resources, email me at thetangledball@gmail.com.

67892982R00089

Made in the USA
Lexington, KY
25 September 2017